I0225531

The Whigs Unmask'd

BEING THE

Secret History

OF THE

Calves'-Head Club

SHEWING

The Rise and Progress of That Infamous Society Since the Grand Rebellion.

CONTAINING

All the Treasonable Songs and Ballads, Sung as ANTHEMS by Those Saints, at Their King-Killing Anniversaries.

Much Enlarg'd and Improv'd by a Genuine Account of All the Plots and Conspiracies of the Whiggish Faction against the QUEEN and Ministry, Since the Persecution of the Church Under the Disguise of *MODERATION*. With Animadversions in Prose and Verse.

Adorn'd with Cuts Suitable to Every Particular Design

To Which Are Added,

Several CHARACTERS by Sir *John Denham*, and Other Valuable Authors.

ALSO

A Vindication of the ROYAL MARTYR, King CHARLES the First; Wherein Are Expos'd, the Hellish Mysteries of the Old Republican Rebellion. By Mr. *Butler*, Author of *Hudibras*.

London
Spradabach Publishing
2023

Spradabach Publishing
BM Box Spradabach
London WC1N 3XX

*The Whigs Unmask'd,
Being the Secret History
of the Calves'-Head Club*

First Spradabach edition published 2023

Interior design by Alex Kurtagic

ISBN 978-1-909606-37-1

British Library Cataloguing-in-Publication Data:
A catalogue record for this book is available from the British Library.

Table of Contents

Note on This Edition

he present is volume is based on the eighth edition of Edward Ward's *The Whigs Unmask'd*, published in London in 1713, the text of which is here reproduced in its entirely.

The spelling and punctuation, have been left as in the original, except where there was a comma or semicolon inside a closing parenthesis (these have been placed outside); and the name of the club, which the author spelt Calves'-Head Club, rather than Calves'-Head Club. The capitalisation has also been left as in the original, except in the chapter titles and section headers, where the capitalisation has been brought into line with modern conventions. Finally, the the Italics are as in the original, except with the song lyrics and Ward's epistle, which have been rendered in Roman type, and where an author's name appeared italicised, followed by the title of one of his works in Roman type; in such instances, to avoid confusion, the author's name has been rendered in roman type and the book title in italics. Minor typographical errors have been silently corrected.

A complement of editiorial footnotes has been added and identified as such to distinguish them from authorial footnotes, and a comprehensive index has been generated.

An

EPISTLE

TO THE

Worthy Members

OF THE

Calves'-Head Club

Worthy Patrons,

ou will not take it amiss, I hope, that I venture to make you the *Patrons* of this new Edition of the following Sheets, when I have honestly told you my Reasons for so doing. I need not inform you that they were writ and publish'd at first purely to do you service, and the Collection made from your own *Memoirs*; and indeed I must own, I am very much at a stand what *Apology* to make for you, that after so many *Publications* they should have no better effect.

In the few things I intend to offer to you I shall be very plain, and therefore you must grant me your Pardon, that in making my Court to you I avoid the usual Complements of formal *Addressors*. There are some of your Society, I am sensible, are Persons of no mean *Abilities*; and to those I shall only take the liberty to say, that 'tis the Subject both of my Wonder and Sorrow, that they should suffer their private *Resentments* so far to lessen their *Characters*, and betray them into such scandalous and contemptible *Conversation*.

As to you, *Gentlemen*, that are the *Common Riotors* of the Day, I confess I want Words to express myself to you. 'Tis true nothing holds Poyson like the Hoof of an Asse, and certainly the *Metaphor* can never be better apply'd than in your Case: Nothing but the thickness of an *Antimonarchical Skull* could contain such Venomous Principles, Principles so directly opposite to all manner of Moral Goodness and Humanity.

But as my Design, in this new *Publication*, is, chiefly, to expose your Folly, and thereby bring you off from a *Practice*, that must, undoubtedly, terminate in your Destruction, I cannot suspect but that you'll make the proper use of it, and instead of furnishing me with new Matter against the next *Thirtieth of January*, you will, at your general *Meeting*, dissolve your Society, and so save me the trouble of any more *Editions*, which you may, otherways, solemnly expect.

Come, my Worthy *Patrons*, for once, give me leave to speak freely to you; You have form'd a *scandalous Society*; and, in Contempt of the *Law*, the *Monarchy*, and the Solemnity of the Day, you meet, eat *CALVES-HEADS*, drink *Rebellious* Healths, and sing your *Seditious Songs* and *Ballads*; and pray, for what purpose is all this? Would you destroy the *Constitution*, and put us again upon a FORTY ONE Bottom? and truly, *Gentlemen*, this must be the very Case, or else you are a *Set* of stubborn inconsiderate *Blockheads*, and are only acted by a Spirit of Contradiction .

In all the Accounts of humane Actions, there is not one Instance of such an *execrable Villany. A King, the best of Kings* (in contradiction to all the Laws of the Nation) forc'd to a *Tryal*, and Condemn'd by a few *Rebellious Scoundrels*; and, to make the Villany still greater, *Executed at the Gate of his own Palace.* An Act that all *Ages* and *Kingdoms* will abhor to the End of the World; and is it in Commemoration of this you eat your *CALVES-HEADS*, and sing your *blasphemous Songs* and *Anthems*?

I protest, if the Matters of Fact were not so fully prov'd upon you, I should no more believe there could be such a Crew of *desperate Miscreants* in humane Shapes, than I could, that any Government would suffer such Affronts with Impunity.

Methinks common Policy should guide you a little in this particular, you see your *Party* that was lately so Great and Formidable, is now sunk to nothing, and your most exalted *Patriots* and *Abettors* grown almost below the Contempt of the *Rabble*; and what, in the Name of *Prudence*, is it you expect?

You have try'd all your Arts and *Stratagems* to disturb the *Government*, *circumvent the Peace*, and lessen and traduce the present *Ministers*, and all, you see, is to no purpose: For shame, reflect seriously upon the Hazards you expose yourselves to, and prevent 'em before it be too late: Justice is slow, but the Hands are Iron, and you may depend upon it, these wicked *Practices* will, at sometime or other, bring you under the *Resentment* of the *Government*, and then you're undone.

Come, Patrons, I am your *Friend*, notwithstanding this *Publication*, and I deal so plainly with you. The *Whigs*, and your Factious Corespondents may suggest strange Matters to you. They may amuse you and the *People*, with *Pretender* and *Popery*, and fill their Heads full of Mighty Things from A broad, but, take my Word, is all mere Delusion. Their *Plots* are all discover'd and defeated, and their *Foreign Friends* are utterly unable to assist them; so that all that they can hope for now, is an Acts of Indemnity; which, to tell you the truth, unless they mend their Manners, I think they very ill deserve.

I shall not trouble you now, with my Opinion concerning the Performances in the following Sheets, they are vouch'd to me, as Genuine and Authentick, and you are the best Judges whether they are or not; for your sakes', indeed, I could wish they were spurious, but that will require very strong Proofs, on your side, which, I'm afraid, you won't think proper to produce one, so I'll e'en let that Matter stand as it does.

And thus, Worthy *Patrons*, I have told you my Thoughts, and done as the *Thracians* of old us'd to do with their drunken *Helots*, expos'd you to the *Publick*, that the *People* may be nauseated by your vile and detestable Practices. Whether you will think me worthy your Patronage or not, is no great matter. I have, at worst, this Satisfaction, that the Papers are intended to convert you, and divert others; and if I succeed in either, I gain my Point. Who am,

Your Humble Servant.

The

PREFACE

he following Collection has been so industriously handed up and down, where it was thought it would be well received, and confirm those Principles which too many have unhappily sucked in, and raise the Confidence of those who were thought too bashful for their Party, that some honest Men have thought, that there could be no more effectual Remedy for the Mischief it might do, or any surer way to stop the Career, than a Publication: For tho' many may presume, that under the Disguise of Mirth, and the Protection of a free Conversation, they might safely venture to make an Experiment, how far the Poyson would work upon the Undiscerning of untry'd Constitutions, especially when Rhime and Musick were he Vehicles, and, under the Rose, was the Word; yet it is believed, when the Malignity of the Draught is publickly discover'd, few will venture upon it with nut a sufficient Antidote; and fewer have the hardiness to administer it.

These Lines for such Ribbaldry and Trash, deserve not the Name of Poems) were compos'd and set to Musick, for the Use of the CALVES'-HEAD CLUB, which was erected by an impudent Sett of People, who have their Feast of Calves-Heads in several Parts of the Town, on the *Thirtieth of January*, in Derision of the Day, and Defiance of Monarchy; at divers of which Meetings, the following Compositions were sung, and in Affront to the Church, call'd *Anthems*. These which are here published, are said to have been written by Mr. *Benj. Bridgewater*, and that he was largely rewarded by the Members of the CLUB for his Pains. Whether Mr. Stevens was so well gratify'd for his Sermons to the Same Tune, and on the Same Days, is more than the Publisher dares say; but perhaps the Pulpit was a Bar to his Pretentions, and the Poet had been better rewarded than the Preacher, had his Sermons been put into Rhime.

However, it is hoped, that this Publication may give a Check to the Evil of the Example, and destroy the Continuance of the Practice, or, at least, give fair Warning, and take away the Pretence of Surprize from those, who shall proceed to insult the Government in so Saucy and so villainous a Manner.

But, whatever the Success may be, the Publisher doubts not but his Intentions are justify'd, and wishes the Effect may demonstrate the Reasonableness of them, by putting an end to so unchristian and scandalous a Practice.

The Whigs Unmaskd:

OR, THE

SECRET HISTORY

OF THE

Calves'-Head Club,

Shewing the Rise and Progress of That Infamous Society

'is a prodigious Thing to consider, (and for the Honour of my native Country, I wish I could say it was a false Imputation upon her) that the *execrable Regicides* of King *Charles* the First, should find any Advocates or Abettors still among us.

I say, 'tis prodigious, that after the whole Nation, by their Representatives in Parliament assembled, have enacted so solemn a Detestation of this unnatural Parricide, and appointed a Day of Humiliation for it, to continue to all Ages of the World, there should be such a Set of *Boutefews* yet remaining, so impudently audacious, as to justify a

Crime, for which the Three Kingdoms have smarted so severely; and in their wicked Merriment, to rehearse as much as in them lies, that tragical Scene, which has justly made us infamous in the remotest Corners of the Universe.

Was it not enough, that a powerful Prince, ally'd to most of the *Crown'd Heads* in *Christendom*, should be despoil'd of that just Authority, wherewith the Laws of *God* and *Man* had invested him, and lastly, of his *Life*; but that he must be most barbarously persecuted after his Death, and suffer those Indignities in his *Memory*, when *dead*, which he had so plentifully suffer'd in his *Person*, when *living?*

There is a time when the most implacable Malice is satiated, and exerts itself no longer. The most savage Nations seldom or never carried their Resentments beyond the Grave; and thought it a piece of barbarous Cowardice to insult upon the *Ashes* that could not speak for themselves.

But the *Royal Martyr* has been treated, if 'tis possible, with more Inhumanity after his Dissolution, than he was exposed to when under the Power of his Rebellious Subjects: He has not only been stigmatiz'd by the odious Name of *Tyrant*, who was, in truth, the best and most *merciful Father* of his *Country*, and loaded with a thousand Calumnies; but, to shew the restless Malice of his Adversaries, even that incomparable *Book of Devotion*, compos'd by him in his Solitude, and the time of his deepest Afflictions, and which no Pen but his own could have written, has been adjudg'd as a spurious Imposition upon the Publick, by a late *Mercenary Author*;[1] altho' 'tis certain to all such Men as can distinguish Stiles, that the Person, to whom the Republicans ascribe it, was no more capable of writing so excellent a Piece, than the aforesaid Compiler of Milton's *Life*, of penning an Orthodox System of the *Mysteries of Christianity*.

Thus, as he was torn from his *Queen* and *Children* in his *Life*, he was *Robb'd*, as far as it lay in the Power of his malicious Enemies, even of the legitimate Issue of his Brain; but as Truth, when dead, especially Truth injuriously oppress'd, never wants some generous Hand to defend its Cause; so all the Arguments that have been used by the *Republicans*, to prove it spurious have been fully answer'd by a worthy[2] *Divine* now living, beyond all Possibility of a Reply.

Neither did the Barbarity of his Enemies stop here; for not content to have *Assassinated* his *Person* and *Reputation*, they even dispossessed him of his *Sepulchre*, (a picce of Cruelty, which none but such thorow-pac'd *Villains* ever executed) for when the long *Parliament*[3] had voted an

1 See Toland's *Life of Milton*. [John Toland, *The Life of Milton* (London: John Darby, 1699). —Ed.]

2 Dr. WAGSTAFF.

3 See Dr. NALSON's Preface to the King's Tryal. [*A True copy of the journal of the High Court of Justice for the tryal of K. Charles I as it was read in the House of Commons and attested under the hand of Phelps, clerk to that infamous court / taken by J. Nalson Jan. 4, 1683 : with a large introduction* (Thomas Dring, 1684). —Ed.]

Honourable Interment for their late *Prince*, who had suffer'd so unjustly, they were disappointed, by reason that the Persons order'd to regulate the Ceremony, when they came to examine the Royal Coffin, found the Body missing.

This puts me in mind of what a worthy *Gentleman*, who travell'd with my Lord *A*_____ into *Italy*, told me some Years since, *viz.* That during his short Stay at *Bern* in *Switzerland*, a Syndic of the Town, who used frequently to visit Major General *Ludlow*, when he lived in those *Parts*, assured him, that he had often heard *Ludlow*, in a vaunting manner affirm, That tho' *Ireton* and *Cromwel* were buried under *Tyburn*, yet 'twas a Comfort to him, that the *Royal Martyr* kept them Company; for, says he, foreseeing that his *Son* would undoubtedly come in, we took care that his *Father's Body* should not be Idolatrously Worshipped by the *Cavaliers*; and therefore privately remov'd it to the place of Common Execution.

Whether the impudent Affirmation of *Ludlow* be true or false, 'tis not material here to enquire, tho' I think nothing can give any honest Man a juster and greater Aversion to the Libertines of that Party, than to observe, that they desire their Malice should be thought without Bounds, and that it neither spares the Dead nor the Living.

But of all the Indignities offer'd to the *Manes* of this injur'd *Prince*, nothing, in my Opinion, comes up to the Inhumanity and Prophaneness of the *Calves'-Head Club*.

For my part, I was of Opinion at first, That the Story was purely contriv'd on purpose to render the *Republicans* more odious than they deserv'd; for I could not imagine how any Party of Men, that pretended to be *Christians*, or that call'd themselves *English*, could calmly and sedately applaud an Action, condemn'd not only by the Word of GOD, but by the Laws of the Land, to which they verbally pay so great a Deference.

As for the *Regicides*, who were actually concern'd in this *execrable Tragedy*, this may be said, however, in favour of them, (if I may be allowed so to express myself towards Criminals of that Magnitude) that having gone so far in their Wickedness, and given His *Majesty* such insupportable Provocations, and, what is more, measuring his Clemency by their own Cruelty, they concluded he could never forgive them; and therefore, like *Cataline*, found themselves under the necessity of committing greater Crimes, in order to cover themselves from the Infamy of what was past.

But what can be offer'd to extenuate the Crime of these *Atheistical Miscreants*, who make that a Matter of their lewd Mirth, which the whole Nation has in the most solemn manner, ever since lamented; and over their Cups to applaud the most wicked Action which the Sun ever beheld?

For this Reason, my good Nature made me look upon it as a Fiction upon the Party, 'till happening, in the late *Reign*, to be in the Company of a certain *active Whig*, who in all other Respects, was a Man

A Description of the Calve's Head Club

of Probity enough, and he assured me, that, to his Knowledge, 'twas true, affirming also, that he knew most of the *Members* of the *Calves'-Head Club*, and that he had been often invited to their *Meetings*, but had always avoided them; adding, that according to the Principles he was bred up in, he would have made no Scruple to have met *Charles* the First in the Field, and oppos'd him to the utmost of his Power; but that since he was dead, he had no farther Quarrel to him, and looked upon it as a cowardly piece of Villany, below any Man of Honour, to insult upon the Memory of a Prince, who had suffer'd enough in his Life-time.

He farther told me, that *Milton*, and some other Creatures of the Commonwealth, had instituted this *Club*, as he was inform'd, in Opposition to Bp. *Juxon*, Dr. *Sanderson*, Dr. *Hammond*, and other *Divines* of the Church of *England*, who met privately every 30th of *January*; and tho' it was under the Time of the *Usurpation*, had compil'd a private Form of Service for the Day, not much different from what we now find in the *Liturgy*.

That after the Restauration the Eyes of the Government being upon the whole Party, they were obliged to meet with a great deal of Precaution; but now, lays he, (and this was the second Year of King *William*'s Reign) they meet almost in a publick Manner, apprehending no Danger.

By another Gentleman, who, about eight Years since, went out of Curiosity to see their *Club*, and has since furnish'd me with the following Papers,

I was informed that it was kept in no fix'd House, but that they remov'd as they thought convenient; and that the Place they met in, when he was with 'em, was in a blind Alley near *Moorfields*, where an Axe hung up in the *Club-Room*, and was reverenced as a principal Symbol in this Diabolical Sacrament. Their Bill of Fare, was a large Dish of *Calves-Heads*, dressed several ways, by which they represented the King and his Friends, who had suffer'd in his Cause; a large Pike with a small one in his Mouth, as an Emblem of Tyranny; a large *Cod's-Head*, by which they pretended to represent the Person of the King singly; a Boar's-Head with an Apple in its Mouth, to represent the King, by this, as Beastial, as by their other Hieroglyphicks they had done Foolish and Tyrannical. After the Repast was over, one of their Elders presented an *Ikon Basilike*, which was with great Solemnity burn'd upon the Table, whilst the *Anthems* were singing. After this, another produc'd *Milton's Defensio Populi Anglicani*, upon which all laid their Hands, and made a Protestation in form of an Oath, for ever to stand by, and maintain the same. The Company wholly consisted of *Independants* and *Anabaptists*, (I am glad, for the Honour of the *Presbyterians*, to set down this Remark;) and that the famous *Jerry White*, formerly Chaplain to *Oliver Cromwel*, who, no doubt came to sanctify with his pious *Exhortations*, the *Ribaldry* of the *Day*, said *Grace*; that after the *Table-Cloth* was re moved, the Anniversary *An-*

them, as they impiously call'd it, was sung, and a *Calf's-Skull* fill'd with Wine, or other Liquor, and then a Brimmer went about to the *pious Memory* of those worthy Patriots who had kill'd the *Tyrant*, and deliver'd their Country from his *arbitrary Sway*; and lastly, a Collection was made for the *Mercenary* Scribler, to which every Man contributed according to his Zeal for the Cause, and Ability of his Purse.

I have taken Care to set down what the Gentleman told me, as faithfully as my Memory would give me leave; and I am perswaded,that some Persons that frequent the *Black Boy* in *Newgate-Street*, as they knew the Author of the following Lines, are well satisfy'd that this Account of the *Calves'-Head Club*, is no fictitious Imposition.

Now, I will appeal to any unprejudiced *English-man*, whether such *shameful Assemblies* ought not to be suppressed with utmost Diligence, and prosecuted with Severity?

Let us consider them either in Relation to the Christian Religion we profess, or to common Humanity and good Manners, or lastly, to the Laws of the Land, and we cannot but allow they affront all equally.

Therefore I hope the *Magistrates* and others, whom it concerns, will take Care, especially now, since they have the Countenance of the Government, to prohibit, as far as in them lies, and detect these wicked Meetings, that the Persons there assembling, may be punish'd as they deserve.

Tho' no Man abominates Persecution more than myself, yet I will venture to say, that a Set of People, who wish the Subversion of our *Ecclesiastical* and *Civil* Establishment, (as appears by the following Papers the Fanaticks do) ought to expect no Quarter from our Hands.

A Song on the 30th of *January*, 1690

I.

Now let's sing, carouse and roar,
The happy Day is come once more
For to Revel,
Is but civil,
As our Fathers did before;
Who, when the Tyrant would enslave us,
Chopp'd his Calf's-Head off to save us.

II.

Let each Youth his Love forsake,
And a merry Bumper take;
Let no Round-Head
Here be grounded,
And drink dry the French-Man's Lake:
Thus in Clarret me caress us,
Till old Puss awake and bless us.

III.

Let the Prelates now go on,
And rail afresh at Forty One,
The deposing
They're 'spousing,
We the Father, they the Son.
Through the Treason, they did find us,
They, my Friends, are not behind us,

IV.

Then let's Laugh and Revel here,
And of our Calf's-Head make good Chear,
This we Dish up,
And no Bishop
Dines without one all the Year:
Thus we prosper without fighting;
In Practice and in Food uniting.

Reflections on a Song on the 30th of *January*, 1690.

Fall the *Balladian Smithfield* Jingles, that ever any persecuted Ear underwent the Penance of, the foregoing Madrigal is certainly the poorest Stuff, for besides the Impudence and Scurility so plentifully diffus'd thro' every Stanza thereof, the Incoherence is so great, and the Nonsense so inimitable, that the Stupidity of the Author, ought to stand registered in his Works, behind every House of Office Door, belonging to those Houses, where their inhuman Feasts have been so impudently solemniz'd .

The Reader may observe in this, as well as most of their other *Ballads*, that their Malice is not only levell'd at the Monarch, but equally at the Church; for Bishops, as well as Kings, they all along make the Subjects of their venomous Scurrility; so that the very Blessings they seem to hope for by a Subversion, both of Church and State, can be no other than the Liberty of Sinning, without Penalty or Punishment; and the Property of robbing honest Men of their Rights, without being call'd to an account for it.

An Anniversary Anthem, 1693

Once more, my Muse, resume thy chear Lyre,
Let this Day's Acts eternal Thoughts inspire;
Let every smiling Glass with Mirth be crown'd,
While Healths to England's native Rights go Round
One such another Day as this alone,
Would fully for a Nation's Sin attone.
'Tis a sure symptom that the People's bless'd,
When once a haughty Tyrant's dispossess'd.

Chorus

Apollo's pleas'd, and all the tuneful Nine
Rejoice, and in the solemn Chorus join,

II.

Again, my Muse, immortal Brutus sing,
Whose daring Sword expel'd a Tyrant King:
Then bravely fought, and bravely overcame,
To give Rome freedom, and eternal Fame.
Such force bas Liberty, such cond'ring-Charms
That the whole World submitted to their Arms.
What Wreaths shall we prepare, and how rebearse
His lasting Worth in everlasting Verse?

Chorus

Apolo's pleas'd, &c.

III.

Triumphant Laurels too must crown that Head
Whose righteous Hand struck England's Tyrant dead:
The Heroes too, adorn'd with Blood and Sweat
Who forc'd the opposing Monster to retreat.
Heaven still before a leading Angel sent;

They conquer'd cause; they an his Errand went
Like the Israelites of old, their Chains they broke,
Guided by Pillars both of Fire and Smoke.

CHOR.

Apollo's pleas'd, &c.

IV

'Tis Force must pull a lawless Tyrant down;
But give Men Knowledge and the Priest's
undone.
When once the lurking Poyson is descry'd,
His juggling Tricks are all in vain appl'd.
In vain be Whines, in vain he Cants and Prays,
There's not a Man believes one Word he says.
'Tis true, Religion is the grand Pretence;
But Power and Wealth's the Mythologick sense.

CHOR.

Apollo's pleas'd, &c.

V

Then fill the longing Glass with spritely Wine,
Our Cause is Justice, and the Health's Divine.
The Heroes smile, and our Delights approve,
Which adds new Joys to those they find
above:

'Twas so they Honour, so they Conquest
sought;
Thus fairly Drank, and then as fairly fought.
They love to see us thus our Homage pay,
And bless the just Occasion of the Day.

CHOR.

Apollo's pleas'd, &c.

Reflections on an Anniversary Anthem, Sung at the *Calves'-Head Club*, on the 30th of January, 1693

The diabolical Principles, and inveterate Malice of these rebellious Miscreants cannot well be render'd more odious to the Publick, than they are made appear by themselves, in the first Stanza of the foregoing Anthem, as they impudently call it; wherein they most wickedly desire to be *eternally inspir'd* with the fame *Blood-thirsty Thoughts* that mov'd their villanous Predecessors to perpetrate that barbarous Murder, which they so Hellishly committed upon the best of Princes; and to further shew what an irreconcilable Hatred they have to our *English* Constitution, *viz.* Monarchical Government, in the fifth Line of the same Stanza, they are so far from looking upon their past Cruelty to the Royal Martyr, to be sinful and abominable, that they wish *for such another Day, to attone for the Sins of the Nation*: As if Innocent and Royal Blood, shed by the vile Hands of rebellious Murderers, could be an acceptable Sacrifice to Heaven, in order to appease the Wrath of the Divine Majesty, for our Wickedness against him. Good GOD! what Devils in Human Shape must those accursed Wretches be, who dare to blaspheme Heaven with such Infernal Suggestions, and blacken their Creator's Image with such damnable provoking Principles, which ought, with out a publick Recantation, to be punished with Death in this world, and doubtless will, without a cordial Repentance, be severely rewarded with Damnation in the next.

In Stanza the third, the Reader may observe, with what audacious Insolence they extol the infamous Hand of the transcendant Villain, who gratify'd their Malice with that execrable Stroke, which the most barbarous Executioner would have trembled at the fight of, and have startled at an Importunity to have perform'd, not only so cruel, but so desperate an Office.

This Poem being all of a Piece, it would have prov'd but a dull Talk to have remark'd more of its Particulars, be cause the Poet after, in every Stanza, harps much upon the same String.

Anniversary Anthem, 1694

I.

The Storm is blown over, the Tempest is past,
The Tyrant is fallen, and is conquer'd at last.
Our Fathers resolv'd it, and bravely 'twas done,
To Save the whole Kingdom by lopping the Crown.
By her Looks, we discover'd the Nation was pleas'd;
Her Fears were all vanish'd, her Troubles were eas'd.
Whilst we Yearly commend an Attempt so Divine,
And applaud the just Action with Calf's-Head and Wine.

CHORUS

II.

Thus Rome, when she suffer'd by seven lewd Kings,
That shackled her Freedom, and pinion'd her Wings,
Long times he sat mournful, as England had done,
And bow'd to the Weight of a Tyrannous Throne;
'Till urg'd with new Griefs, she for Liberty cry'd,

And Liberty round the glad Echo reply'd;
Whilst *Brutus* resolv'd to give *Tarquin* his
Doom,
And offer a King to the Welfare of Rome.

Chorus

III.

When by Tyrants Endeavours the People are
prest,
Let this noble Example inspire e'ery Breast
With the same Resolutions to defend the
Good Cause,
The Subjects just Rights, their Religion and
Laws.
Then fill the Calf's Cranium to a Health so
Divine,
The Cause, the old Cause shall enoble our
Wine;
Charge briskly around, fill it up, fill it full,
'Tis she last and best Service of a Tyrannick
Scull.

IV.

Then, Boys, let's drink a Bumper, since their
Actions made us great,
Let us lay our Trophies at their Feet:
The Cause gave Courage to the Soldiers,
taught them how their Foes to beat,

That alone could free a captiv'd State.

V.

Then to Puss, Boys, to Puss, Boys,
Let's drink it off thus Boys,
As our Fathers did, and the World shall us
adore;
It's happier to die, Boys,
Than in Slavery to lie Boys;
Thus the Heroes chose it, and bravely dy'd
before.

Reflections on an Anniversary Anthem, Sung at the *Calves'-Head Club* the 30th of *January*, 1694

The Drift of their rhyming Secretary, I find, in all his rebellious *Ballads*, which (instead of *Anniversary Anthems*) I think they ought to have been call'd, is much the same, with very little Variation of Thought, tho', in his Measure, I must confess there is some Variety which, I suppose, was principally owing to the Difference of the Tunes, scandalizid with their rebellious Poetry; for finding (as I suppose) no Musician in the Town, that would degenerate so far from his own harmonious Nature, as to herd with such an infamous Society, who, like Imps and Furies, delight in nothing but Discord and Confusion, they were forc'd to dishonour some old Tunes or other, with their in harınonical Bombast, which might be a Disadvantage to their King-killing *Anthem* maker, who, if he had understood Musick, it would have certainly soften'd his Nature, and reform'd his Principles, as well as his Poetry, that he would have scorn'd to have made himself so infamous an Author.

In the first Stanza of the foregoing *Anthem*, after (as in all the rest) he has wickedly applauded the Murder of King *Charles* the First; in the last two Lines there is great Satisfaction given to all such Persons, who, through the Honesty of their own Principles, and an utter Abhorrence of the Treasonable Barbarity aforemention'd, could not believe, that among Human Race, there could be found such an Impious Society of incorrigible Rebels, that should dare to provoke Heaven, and shame Earth, by keeping up a joyful *Anniversary* upon' so dreadful an Occasion. But all such Persons, who, thro' their Charity to Mankind, have been hitherto unwilling to believe there is any such wicked Cabal as the *Calves'-Head Club*, annually solemniz'd upon the 30th of *January*, by a pack of King-killing Villains, may be convinc'd, in their own Words, which in the foregoing Song are pointed to by a Hand, so that a Recital is unnecessary.

In the first Line of the second Stanza their Author is pleas'd to give the Epithet of *Lewd*, to all the seven *Roman Kings*, tho' we cannot find, by History, it was due to any, but to Tarquin; but all

Kings are to him a like Criminal, for amongst such bad Men, none are accounted Good that bear the Royal Title.

In the beginning of his *Anthem*, he mimicks a Song in the *Innocent Adulterer*, call'd, (*viz.*) *The Danger is over*, and concludes it with the transpoſition of another Song, (*viz.*) *Come, Boys, let's fill our Helmets*, &c.

An Anniversary Anthem, 1695, 1698, and 1699

I.

What the Devil means all this Pother
On this Day, more than another?
See! the Sot to Church reels out,
  See! the Leacher leaves his Whore;
  The Rogues, that never pray'd before,
Are grown most plaguily Devout.

II.

Prethee, Parson, why those Faces,
Pious Frowns, and damn'd Grimaces?
Why so many Creeds and Masses,
  Colleets, Lessons, and the rest
  Of the Holy Garbidge drest,
Proper food for mumbling Alles?

III.

Oh! Sir, it's a Debt, they say,
Mother Church must yearly pay
To her Saint's Canonization:
  It was the Day in which he fell
  ☞ A Martyr to the *Cause of Hell*,
Justly crown'd with Decollation.

IV.

Mirth for us and generous Wine;
Let the Clergy cant and whine,
Preach and prate about Rebellion;
  ☞ *No more Beasts of K__'s, good Heaven!*
  Such as late in Wrath were given,
Two curs'd Tyrants and a Stallion.

V.

May the Banish'd Tarquins Fate,
Be as Just, but not so Great;
Some mean shameful Death attend him:
  May Curs'd Lewis, for Old Scores,
  Turn him poorly out of Doors;
Then may some friendly Halter end him .

VI.

Now prepare, my Lads, and stud
Each his Bumper in his Hand.

Brutus! 'tis a Health to thee,
  Thou whose generous Arm and Sword,
  In a Cause like ours, restor'd
Rome's expiring Liberty,

VII.

Fill the Glass with sparkling Red,
Look, 'twas the Tyrant bled .
Thus our Fathers let us see
  What before had Sacred food,
  Fawn'd and worshipp'd as a God,
Was Flesh and Blood, as well as we.

Reflections on an Anniversary Anthem, Sung at the Calves'-Head Club, on the 30th of January, 1695, &c.

To shew what Atheistick Enemies these King-killing Miscreants are to Religion, and all spiritual Order and Discipline, as well as to our Civil Government, their prophane Laureat is not only encourag'd to a constant Vindication of the treasonable Cruelty of their Fathers towards their just and lawful Prince; but in the foregoing Anthem, his blasphemous Raptures are levell'd at the Church, to the Reproach of Heaven, God's Holy Truths, and the Ministers thereof.

In the first Stanza, he has the Impudence to stigmatize the most devout Members of the Church of

England, (who, thro' a just Duty both to God and their King, bear a pious Abhorrence of all King-killing Principles) with the infamous Epithets of *Sots, Lechers, Rogues*, &c. such abominable Usage, that scarce the worst of Scoundrels, except their own wicked Society, and those who justify their Principles and Proceedings, could ever deserve.

In the second Stanza, our Liturgy is complimented with the Name of *Mass*, a usual Contempt which her Rival Saints cast upon the *Common-Prayer-Book*. The Collects and Lessons, which are God's own Words, by his Holy Prophets and Apostles, are blasphem'd with the odious Title of *Garbidge, proper food for mumbling Asses*. Which prophane Expression, shews how far so wicked a Scribe will degenerate from true Wit, to vent his Malice and Impiety; for I believe it was never known, that *Garbidge* was held *proper Food for Asses*.

In the third Stanza, they have the Impudence to stile the King's Heroick Sufferings, for the Preservation of the Dignities of the Crown to his Posterity, the Laws of the Land, the Liberties of the People, the just Constitution of Parliaments, and the establish'd Church, *fallen for the Cause of Hell*. Oh! execra ble Monsters!

In the fourth Stanza, observe with what malicious, rude, and impious Devotion, he offers up a prophane Prayer to Heaven, reproaching Kings, who are God's Vicegerents, with the scurrilous Name of *Beasts*, and branding a Succession of three, as Heroick Princes as ever sat upon the *English* Throne, or any other, with the malicious Accusation of being *Cursed Tyrants*, of which Charge none but such incorrigible Rebels could ever say, that either of them were guilty.

In the fifth Stanza, the Reader may observe how far these unmerciful Regicides are degenerated from those Christian Principles that bind us to an Universal Charity for all Mankind, which ought to extend even to those we take to be our greatest Enemies; and how they are also poyson'd with Inveteracy to such a Degree, that they are utterly divested of that Compassion and Humanity, which, in all Ages, has been valu'd and pre serv'd amongst the greatest Heathens, or otherwise these barbarous Rebels could never pray, that the most unfortunate of Princes, depos'd, banish'd, and render'd wholly unable to oppose their Villanies, should by his only Friend *be turn'd poorly out of Doors*, and that he should have no Rufuge, but a Halter to put an End to his Misfortunes. Oh! the admirable Christian Charity of these tender-hearted Monsters!

The two following Stanza's are stuff'd only with the same Ribaldry, which thcir Poet uses in all his Songs, so that there is nothing in them worth speaking to.

An Anthem on the 30th of January, 1696

There was a King of *Scottish* Race,
A Man of muckle Might a,
Was never seen in Battles great,
But greatly be would Sh____a;
This King begot another King,
Which made the Nation sad a,
Was of the same Religion,
An Atheist, like his Dad a:
This Monarch wore a picked Beard,
And seem'd a doughty Heroe,
As *Dioclesian* Innocent, and as Merciful as Nero.
The Church's darling Implement,
But Scourge of all the People;
He swore he'd make each Mother's Son
Adore their Idol Steeple:
But they perceiving bis Designs,
Grew plaguy shy and jealous,
☞ And timely chopt his *Calf's-Head* off
And sent him to his Fellows.
Old Rowly did succeed bis Dad,
Such a King was never seen a,
He'd lie with ev'ry nasty Drab,
But seldom with his Queen a.
Restless and hot be roll'd about
The Town, from Whore to Whored,
A merry Monarch as e'er liv'd,
Yet scandalous and poor a.

His Dogs at Council-Board would for
    Like Judges in their Furs a;
'Twas bard to say which bad most Wit,
    The Monarch, or bis Curs a.
At last he dy'd, we know not how,
    But most think by bis Brother;
His Soul to Royal *Tophes* went,
    To see his Dad and Mother.
The furious *James* usurp'd the Throne,
    To pull Religion down a;
But by bis Wife and Priest undone,
    He quickly lost his Crown to
To *France* the wand'ring Monarch's trudg'd,
    In hopes Relief to find a,
Which he is like to have from thence,
    Ev'n when the D_____'s blind a.
Oh! how should we rejoice and pray,
    And never cease to sing 4,
☞If Bishops too were chas'd away,
    And banish'd with their King a
Then Peacc and Plenty would ensue;
    Our Bellies would be full a,
The enliven'd Isle would laugh and smile,
    As in the Days of *Noll* a.

Reflections on an Anniversary Anthem, Sung at the *Calves'-Head Club* the 30th of *January*, 1696

In this *Anthem*, the Reader may, that their Malice and Aversion is not particularly extended to the Memory of any one Prince, upon the Account of any Mísmanagements they can charge uponone Reign more than another; but that they have imbib'd from the Rebellious Examples of their Fore-Fathers, such an irreconcilable Prejudice to all Kingly Sovereignty, and all Persons who exercise the Royal Authority over them, tho' never so mildly, lawfully, and justly, that they cannot forbear spitting their Venom equally upon the whole Race of Kings, from our first happy Union with *Scotland*, treating them all alike, with such opprobrious Language, that any Person may easily perceive their spiteful Calumnies, odious Lies and Abuses, and their prophane Scurrility, are not only levell'd, I say, at those Princes, whose Faults they have most unjustly magnify'd and multiply'd, but also at the very Power, Dignity, and Office of a King, and all that has a Tendency to the Support of Regal Government; to which they are such avow'd and inveterate Enemies, that nothing but the Danger of the Law re strains their Insolence from offering the like Affronts to Her present Majesty. For since they have the Impudence to use all Her Majesty's Royal Predecessors with such shameful Irreverence, as they do in this Poem, I am sure it is sufficient to convince any reasonable Man, that their Prejudice to so merciful and good a Family, can arise from nothing, but an invincible Hatred to all Monarchy in general, which they consequently turn towards all Persons that exercise a Kingly Authority over them, though never so uprightly.

Besides, the Reader may satisfy himself in the latter end of this Poem, that the Subversion of the Monarchy is not the only thing these Vipers aim at, but the Hierarchy also, well knowing, the one cannot expire without the other, therefore they wish the *Bishops banish'd, and chas'd away with King James, that they may be restor'd to the Blessings of an* Oliverian *Government.* From whose last Words, the Reader is desir'd to observe how inconsistently these rebellious Libertines act to themselves, in celebrating the bloody, tyrannical, and calamitous Reign of the Usurper, who trampled up on that very Republick, of which they boast, (in spite of all their Stratagems, and wrested the Government from their democratical Senate, and plac'd it in Opposition to their Principles, in his own single Person, to the total Overthrow of that Scheme they had all along projected.

An Anthem on *January* the 30th, 1697

I.

Touch, now touch the tuneful Lyre,
  Make the joyful Strings resound;
The Victory's at last intire,
  With the Royal Victim crown'd.

II.

The happy Stroke did soon recover
  What we long bad fought in vain,
Thus *Ariadne* lost her Lover,
  But the Gods reliev'd her Pain,

III.

This was an Action just and daring,
  Nature smil'd at what they did,
When our Fathers, nothing fearing,
  Made the haughty Tyrant bleed.

IV.

They their Sons thus well obliging,
  Taught us how this Day to keep,
Who by fighting, storming, sieging,
  Laid the ravening Wolf asleep,

V.

England long her Wrongs Sustaining,
  Press'd beneath her Burthens down,
Chose a Set of Heroes daring,
  To chastise the haughty Crown.

VI.

Thus the Romans, whose beginning
  From an equal Right did spring,
Abhorring Romulus his sinning,
  To the Gods transfer'd their King.

VII.

Let the Black Guard rail no further,
  Nor blaspheme the righteous Blows
Nor miscall that Justice, Murther,
  Which made Saint, and Martyr too.

VIII.

They and We this Day observing,
  Differ only in one thing
They are canting, whining, starving,
  We rejoicing, drink, and sing.

IX.

Advance the Emblem of the Action,

Fill the Calf's-Scull full of Wine;
Drinking ne'er was counted Faction,
Men and Gods adore the Vine.

X.

To the Heroes gone before us,
Let's renew the flowing Bowl,
Whilst the Lustre of the Glories
Shine like Stars from Pole to Pole.

Reflections on an Anniversary Anthem, Sung at the *Calf's-Head-Chub*, on the 30th of *January*, 1697

T*ouch now the tuneful Lyre*, is the amorous beginning of the foregoing Madrigal; but, in my Conscience, I think the Poet ought rather to have call'd upon some of *Belfegar*'s Musick; for certainly a Lottery-man's Trumpet, or a *Bartholomew*-Fair Carcal would have sympathiz'd much better with such a wicked Roundelay, than so soft and musical an Instrument, as his Infernal Muse has invok'd to her Assistance: For where his Song is in Praise of the most barbarous Villany that ever was perpetrated, sure no Body upon Earth is so fit to be his Minstrel, as the wry-mouth'd Salisbury Fidler that play'd to the Devil and his Imps all the *Christmass* Holy-days.

This piece of Lyrick Poetry, is so true a *Pye-corner* Panegyrick upon their old rebellious Proceedings, and dwells so tediously upon the *Happy Stroke*, as he impudently calls it, and upon the Vertues and Excellencies of those puritanical (Hedghogs, who wounded the Kingdom, with their Prickles, in those confounded Times of Liberty and Property, when a parcel of ravenous Wolves had the keeping of the Sheep, and a pack of yelping Bloodhounds made their Kennels in our Churches, that there is scarce any thing in it that will admit of further Reflections, than what I have already made, except these Passages following.

In the third and fourth Stanzas, the Reader may observe, that they do not only impudently extol the Justice of that daring Action in their Fathers (i.e.) brewing their vile Hands in the Blood of the Blessed Martyr; but they also tell us, that they, (their Sons) are highly oblig'd to their Progenitors *for laying the ravenous Wolf asleep*, and that they are beholding to their *Fathers for teaching them to keep this Day, viz.* the 30*th* of *January*; so that in the first place it is to be noted, that they have drawn the Guilt of all their Fathers Treasons, Murders, and Rebellions, upon their own Heads, by approving, applauding, and so heartily consenting to their Wickedness, *ex post Facto*, and I question not, but they will all live to be punish'd accordingly. In the next placé they acknowledge, that this wicked Anniversary was constituted by their Fathers; and that *their Sons were taught by* *them to observe the same*; so that there is no question to be made, but this abominable Party have kept their Annual Revellings and Rejoicings upon this unfortunate Day, ever since they had the fatal Opportunity of exerting their Cruelty in the King's Martyrdom.

In the seventh Stanza, (which I think is so full of Wickedness, that it could never be paralleld, except by the same Villains) there to shew their Reverence to Religion, they prophanely stigmatize the Loyal and Orthodox Clergy of the best establish'd Church in the World, with the ignominious Name of *Black Guard*, and forbid them by their Railing, *to blaspheme the righteous Blow*: An Expression so hyperbolically wicked, that an honest Man would think nothing could give Vent to such a Hellish Saying, but the very Mouth of a Devil.

His Conclusion is much of the same Strain, wherein the Reader may observe the Temperance and Sobriety of these Fanatical Hypocrites, who, in the Eyes of the World, pretend to so much Grace and Sanctity.

A Song on the 30th of January, 1697. By a Lad of 16

I.

Tune the Lute and Lyre,
Touch the sounding Wyre;
Let our Hearts and Voice
Create such a Noise,
As shall match the Celestial Choir.

II.

Hark! th' exalted Heroes,
Looking on, looking on,
Charm the bright Seraphick Throne,
With Hymns Divine, to cheer us.

III.

The pensive World around us,
Griev'd to see him wound us,
(*a*) But bless'd the Deed,
When they saw him bleed,
Who labour'd to confound us.

IV.

The happy British Isle too,
When she saw, when she saw,

(*b*) The destin'd Head submit to Law,
Began to sing and Smile too.

V.

It was a pleasing Wonder,
Upon the Earth and under;
The Worms beneath
Rejoic'd at his Death,
And gladly fiez'd the Plunder.

VI.

Nought mourns under Heaven,
(*c*) But the Priest, but the Priest,
Whose Hypocrisy's a Jest
Can never be forgiven.

VII.

Hail! Saints Victorious,
(*d*) Who bravely went before us,
Who taught us the way,
When Tyrants sway,
To make a Nation glorious.

VIII.

Thus you give us Freedom,
And Liberty, Liberty,
Shall by your Methods purchas'd be,

Whene'er the People need'em .

IX.

(*e*) The Heroes now in Glory,
Bow themselves before ye,
  Pleas'd to see
  Posterity,
Thus yearly rehearse their Story.

X.

Then fill the Cranium full Boys,
  With sparkling Red, with sparkling Red,
  (*f*) Well knock the sneaking Puppies dead,
Who dare our Mirth controul, Boys.

Reflections on the Foregoing Song on the 30th of January, 1697

Stanza the third, (*a*) with what Impudence would these frantick Republican Monsters insinuate, that the whole World, both approv'd and applauded their unparalleld Villany towards the best of Princes, when it is well known to all good Men, that their Barbarity has been detested by all Kingdoms and States in the Universe, that have ever heard of their Infamy, to the everlasting Shame and Scandal of those Blood-thirsty Hypocrites, who effected their base Ends by such a sanguine piece of Cruelty, to the mildest of Monarchs.

Stanza the fourth, (*b*) observe how they justify their bloody Act, accomplish'd by Rebellion and open Violence, under a Pretence of Law, when their infamous Proceedings were directly repugnant to the Laws of God, the Laws of Nature, and the Laws of the Land.

Stanza the sixth, (*c*) with what Confidence do they charge the Loyal Clergy of the Church of *England*, with that Hypocrisy, which themselves have ever practised, both towards God and Man, to bring their base Designs to their abominable Issue?

Stanza the seventh, (*d*) with what diabolical Presumption they Canonize their Brother Regicides, and confer the holy Dignity of a Saint upon the worst of Murderers.

Stanza the ninth, (*e*) if such a Society of treasonable Ruffians can have the Confidence to fancy their rebellious Progenitors are admitted into Glory, by which they mean Heaven, I must confess the greatest Villain in their whole Party, has but little Reason to despair of future Happiness.

Stanza the tenth, (*f*) you may judge of the excellent Principles of these *Calf's-Head* Liberty and Property Men, from their Words referr'd to, where they are for knocking all good Men on the Head for Puppies, that are for controuling them in their frantick Celebration of that abominable Deed, which no Christians, in their right Senses, can reflect upon, with out Horror and Amazement.

An Anthem on the 30th of *January*.

I.

Welcome, brave Souls,
Now drink off your Bowls,
(*a*) 'Twas an Act we all do admire,
To stifle the Work
Of an *English Turk*,
Whose Son set our City on Fire:

II.

Whose Deeds were forgots
'Till reviv'd by a Plot,
Carry'd on by shitten *Mack-Ninney*:
But the Martyr in Rage,
Lost his Head on a Stage,
(*b*) And the Church swore the Devil was in ye,

III.

Then let us commend
(*c*) The Deeds of a Friend,
That caused our jolly Meeting;
To our Fathers we owe
The Honour o'th' Blow,
And we are their Sons, that are Feasting,

IV.

But who would have thought,
That our *Scotch* Laird
Should make use of the Power of France Sir
But their Work is done,
From Father to Son,
We have lost both Root and Branch, Sir.

V.

Then again let's commend,
That Warlike Hand,
That sav'd our *English* Nation;
'Twas Puss in her Furr,
Did scratol, Spit and purr,
And pointed to Abdication.

Reflections on the foregoing Anthem on the 30th of *January*.

Stanza the first, (*a*) here they are not content to insolently express their Love and Admiration of a barbarous Act, which no good Subject can think on with out Trembling, but even proceed to blast the pious Memory of the most Christian Martyr, with the scurrilous Epithet of *English Turk*; and to basely charge the Fire of *London* upon one of his Sons, (tho' it has been sufficiently prov'd upon their own Party), in order to cast their own Villa-

upon such Persons, who were utterly innocent of the matter.

Stanza the second, (*b*) as themselves say, I think the Church, when they saw the Life of their just and injur'd Monarch so wrongfully and maliciously extorted from him, by the merciless Hands of a parcel of insatiate Rebels, might very justly swear, that the Devil was in 'em; for had he not, it is impossible they should ever have so effectually accomplish'd such a vile and bloody Undertaking.

Stanza the third, (*c*) you may observe in most of their scandalous Ballads, as well as this Stanza, it is the highest of their Vanity, to commend the greatest of their Villanies, and to give abundance of Honour to the Memory of those bloody Assassinators, whose Sons they boast them selves, and that they are proud of the Occasion their Fathers have given them of meeting, to rejoice over the Infamy of their Ancestors. What can a Government expect, but the like Cruelty from the like Party, if they are once again suffer'd to get uppermost?

A Song at the Calves'-Head Club, January the 30th 1698.

I.

Crown, Crown the Goblet, Quaff the sparkling War,
Invoke the Assistance of the Tuneful Nine:

whining, which every Body knows they are ridiculous Qualifications, only practis'd and improv'd by their own dull, spiteful, and illiterate Teachers.

In Stanza the fifth, the Poet after seems mightily pleas'd, to think how the King killers, who he presumes are in Heaven, smile above at the drunken Revels of their rebellious Progeny below: But I doubt he has assign'd a wrong Place for his de fund Patriots, who, in all honest Men's Opinion, are most likely to be found in those dark Regions, where they meet with but little Reason to laugh at the frantick Oblations of their wicked Sons, who succeed them in their Villanies.

An Anniversary Poem on the 30th of January, 1699.

Hail, sacred Day! (*a*) chat each returning
Dost with new Light our drooping Spirits
Remind'st us of our Ancestors Renown,
Who bravely pull'd a (*b*) saucy Tyrant down,
While Liberty Triumphant fill'd the Throne.
The Tydings first at the curs'd Court began,
Which chearfully thro' all the Nation ran:
Fresh streams of unknown Joys around did flow,
And all good Men ador'd the Righteous Blow.
The Sun transported with the noble Deed,
Slone out, and mild to see the Monster bleed.
Th' amaz'd World united in Applause,
And bless'd the Justice of our Arms and Cause.

Nought under Heaven mourn'd but the
curs'd Priest.
Whose damnd Dissimulation is a Jest,
That every free-born Nation should detest.
Thrice hail, illustrious Day! in thee's display'd
Abrighter Scene, than when the World was
When from dark *Chaos* this gay Form was
rear'd,
And all the grizly Phantoms disappeard:
Just so they slunk away, just so they fled,
And groan'd and tumbl'd with the Tyrant's
Head
While general Gladness did the Isle employ,
And every *English* Tongue did shout for Joy:
Hail once again, thou glorious Part of Time!
Thou endless Subject of eternal Rhime!
May I forget to make my Numbers meet,
And tune new Thoughts in well composed Feet.
May she I love, forget to love me more,
Be always wretched, I be always poor,
If I forget this sacred Day t'adore.
When Courage over Slav'ry did prevail,
And Providence weigh'd down the juster Scale;
When Right Triumphant o'er Injustice rode,
Following the Footsteps of the leading God,
Did to the doubting World a Pattern shew,
What *English* Men, for English Rights dare do.

Reflections on an Anniversary. Poem on the 30th of January, 1699

How impudently they prophane the Word *Sacred*, by adding it to the Black Day, which unhappily produc'd the sad Occasion of all our succeeding Miseries! And in Line the fourth, to express their Malice with the greater they Rancour, they stile the best of Kings who was the Object of their Fury, the Sawcy Tyrant; and then, in Line the ninth, to devlishly affirm, that *all good Men ador'd the righteous Blow*, when nothing is more evident, than that none but the worst and wicked est of Men had ever the Impudence to open their Mouths in the Vindication of so base and barbarous a Tragedy. And in the two following Lines, how the Infamous Author seems to be transported with his diabolical Flight! so I may justly term it, for nothing sure but the Fury of Hell, instead of the Muses, could ever have inspir'd, such a Republican Scribler with such an audacious Piece of Bombast, *viz.*

The Sun transported with the noble Deed,
Shone out, and smi'ld to see the Monster bleed.

Indeed the whole Poem is all of a piece, and I think is such a compleat Composition of Malice and Impudence, that none but a *Calves'-Head Club* of the most stigmatiz'd Rebels, would ever have receiv'd under their Villanous Patronage: And as it truly deserves, so I hope it will always remain in Print, as an ever lasting Register of the Author's Shame and Infamy, as well as of the incorrigible Impudence of that vile Society, who at first gave it their Protection.

On the 30th of *January* 1699

Go, cursed Crew, to all Extreams inclin'd
Rough as the Seas; and wav'ring as the Wind,
Too deeply cruel, or too basely kind:
You, like the *Roman* Senate heretofore,
Dead Drink with Superstition, and with Gore,
First Massacre your Monarch, then adore.

A Remark on the Former

When fiery Whigs the Touchwood Land infame
They labour on the Church to cast the Blame;
Thus love the Treason but abhor the Shame.

The Health

When Tories and Parsons do Cant and Pray
And Spit their dull Malice on us,
Let's remember the Cause that occasion'd the Day,
And drink a good Health to Old Puss, Old Puss.
When Priests of Rebellion and Treaso prate;
And extol the lewd Monarch immur'd in the Cake,
Confront 'em with Vagabond *James*'s Fate,
And put 'em in mind of the Stroak they struck;
When Oppression increases, and Hopes grow less,
When Tyrants unbridl'd their Subjects vex,
Let's chear up ourselves with the happy Success,
That once did attend on the Ax, the Ax.
Then Freedom and Peace did in Triumph appear,
As soon as the Glorious Deed was done,
Our Fathers perform'd, and why should we fear.
To follow what they have so well begun?
Moses of old, when the *Jews* despair'd,
How they should threat'ning Dangers shun,
Buoy'd up their Faith with the Wonders they've beard,
Had by their Fathers been done been done;

But we have better Examples instore,
When Power with Liberty won't accord,
Will follow the Pattern they set us before,
And deliver ourselves from the Sword, the
Sword.
Then fill up the Glass to the daring Hand,
Which bravely finish'd the just Design,
And stain'd with Tyrannical Blood the Sand,
While murmuring *Scots* repine, repine.
History of the Calves'-Head Club.
About with't again to the Hand and Cause,
That gave us Occasion to Revel thus;
Confusion to those, who shall dare refuse
To drink a good Health to Old Puss, Old Puss.

Reflections on the Health drank at the Calf's-Head-Feaft

By the *Old Puss*, to which they dedicate their intoxicating Bumpers, I suppose they mean the Good Old Cause; from the farther Promotion of which may Heaven defend Her Majesty and Her Kingdoms; for certainly such audacious Wretches, who have Impudence enough to glory in the vilest Deed that ever was perpetrated by Human Hands, whenever they have Power, will, with as great Joy, repeat the same Villanies and Cruelties, which are so highly approv'd on by their wicked Faction. What can be more startling and amazing to a Man of any Honesty or Conscience, than the unaccountable Insolence of such a daring Society, who, by the damnable Doctrine of their revengeful Teachers, are so harden'd in their Malice against Monarchy and Church-Government, that they should drink to the Memory of that accursed Hand, (over and over, as you find in the foregoing Health) which so barbarously robb'd the best of Princes of his Life, to satisfy the inexorable Revenge of the worst of People? From whose accursed Cruelty, *Good Lord deliver us*.

AN

Appendix

TO THE

Secret History

OF THE

Calves'-Head Club

s the preceeding Anthems were made and sung in the late Reign, when the Party flatter'd themselves with the Connivance of a Prince, who had been bred up in their own Communion; so the Reader may be apt to imagine, that these Practises have been discontinued since Her present Majesty's Accession to the Throne. But to convince him, that neither the Queen's Piety, nor Her unquestion'd Descent from the Loins of the Royal Martyr's Son, neither Her Zeal for the establish'd Church, nor Her Abhorrence of their barbarous Treatment of Her Grandfather's Memory, tho' Her Reign was usher'd in with the Punishment of one *James Taylor*, a Tanner in *Southwark*, who was convicted, and fin'd, and stood in the Pillory, for taking the Freedom to say, *He was us'd no otherwise than he deserv'd, and that it would have been better for the Kingdom if the whole Family* (not excluding Her Majesty) *had been so serv'd*, &c. could keep them within those Bounds of Respect, Subjects ought to be circumscrib'd with. For not holding themselves contented to make use of the Pen, to insinuate evil Surmises of Her Majesty, and Her Ministry's Designs; and of the Tongue, to make Invectives against them in their private Cabals, they rais'd themselves to such a Pitch of Impudence, which they had not arriv'd at, even in the Days of Her Predecessors and openly did that which the good-natur'd sort of People, that have a value for them, are not to be induc'd to believe they would be guilty of in private.

To convince these of the Folly of their Unbelief, among the many Instances that are to be given of their Arrogance and Presumption, I shall lead them no farther off from the present Time, than the 30th of *January* last past, when the Brethren, that call themselves the *Elect*, assembled to give God Thanks at *Salter*'s and *Pinner*'s Halls, for the horrid and cruel Murther of their late dread Sovereign; for the Sequel will make appear, that the manner of celebrating that Black Anniversary, was nothing different from a Day of Rejoicing. The Texts have escap'd my Memory, but the Substance of the Sermon had no Reference to the Fact they should have humbled themselves before God for; and the Portion of Scripture, which was made use of to be sung before Sermon, was the 233 and 24th Verses of the 118*th Psalm*, which are these:

This was the mighty Work of God,
　This was the Lord's own Fact;
And it is wondrous to behold
　With Eyes, that noble Act.
This is the joyful Day indeed,
　Which God himself bath wrought;
Let us be glad, and joy therein,
　In Heart, in Mind, and Thought.

To palliate this, the pretended Saints excuse themselves by the Ignorance of the Clerk, and say, he made choice of the very same Stanza's at the Burial of his own Wife, when her Funeral Sermon was preach'd. But if it was done out of Ignorance, how came the Clerks of the two chief Congregations, *Pinner*'s-Hall, and Salter's-Hall, to make choice of the same Stanza's on the same Occasion? A Man of any Fore sight, must conclude it was concerted between them, and it is not usual for Persons of their Rank, in Conventicles, to do any thing of such a Nature, and in so publick a manner, with out Directions from their Superiors.

Besides, the Management of themselves after Sermon, points out a *Combination*; and that they came not as to the House of Mourning, but the House of Joy: For instead of Fasting, as the Proclamation requir'd, and making Attonement for the

Sins of the Nation, they no sooner broke up their Assembly, but some of the Elders went home with Esquire L_____s, where they were well entertain'd: Amongst other Discourse concerning the Day, the Sermon, and the Psalm, several of the Preachers, who came to this cruel Merry-meeting, were very witty, naming several Texts, as they thought proper for the Occasion, especially one of them, whose Name begins with an S, said, If it had been his turn to have preach'd that Day, he would have chosen for his Text, the Words of Martha to our Saviour, *John* 11. 39. *Lord, by this time be slinketh.*

On the same Day, to shew what Difference a certain Dissenter, not far from *Bartholomew Close*, had for Her Majesty's Proclamation, that was orderd to be read in all Churches and Places of Divine Worship, the Sunday before, set up a Calf's Head upon a publick Place over his Shop or House, to the view of a promiscuous Crowd of Neighbours, who are ready to make Oath of it. But my Reader perhaps may tell me it was no Contempt of the Proclamation in him, since all Proclamations are directed to Her Majesty's *loving Subjects*, and the Dissenters are none of Her Majesty's *loving Subjects*, wherefore it bore no manner of Relation to him.

To crown all, let us take a view of the Faction in the *Burrough* of *Southwark*, and there we shall find them not a Jot behind hand with their Fellow Labourers in Sedition, the Citizens of *London*; and after a plentiful Entertainment at one *Crosley*'s, at the Sign of their two Men, (*viz.* the Two-Brewers) adjourn'd to the *Bull-Head-Tavern*: Among whom was one Mr. *Claxton*, a Gentleman of a fairer Reputation than the rest, whose Occasions calling him down Stairs from the Place of Merriment, gave an Opportunity to one *Mercer*, a Scrivener, to disswade him from returning to his Miscreant Companions, lest Dangers might ensue the Disturbance they made in drinking their abominable Healths, and other Demonstrations of Triumph and Rejoycing. *Claxton* took his Friend's Advice, and went no more to them; but the Drawer, whose Name is *Boise*, and is now a Servant at the same Place, made Affidavit, that they had Fowls for Supper, whose Heads they cut off themselves without doubt to commemorate the Day): and that he observ'd at the drinking of a certain Health, (which was whisper'd about from one to the other, so that the Deponent could not give the Court the Name of it) every other Man laid down his Head upon the Table, and the next Man to him gave a Stroak with his Hand upon his Neck, as if in Imitation of the beloved Act of Decollation; after which follow'd a general *Huzza*; &c. The Noise made a Confusion in the House; by Reason it was altogether improper for such an Anniversary, and the Mistress of the House, upon Enquiry from the Drawer, and the Solicitations of the several other Companies that were refreshing themselves with a Glass, gave notice of it to Justice *Ladd*, a Neighbour of the said *Burrough*, who conven'd them before him, but dismiss'd them for that time, in order to their Appearance before him and the Bench of Justices, when call'd for. Accordingly they were sent for, and examin'd at the next *Session* of the *Peace*, but whether the Law requir'd more direct Proof to convict them, or the Majority of the Gentlemen upon the Bench had not such an Abhorrence of such Principles as they deserv'd, I am not to determine, they were dismiss'd without any Prosecution, which has been thought strange among some People, while Protections of the adverse Party are so much in request.

At another Tavern, in the same Year above mentioned, there were a Company of fowre Whigs got together a Tipling, and discoursing over their Godly Deeds, from Forty One and downwards, they came at last to their *joyful Day indeed*, the Decollation of King *Charles* the First: Upon which, one of them shrugg'd up his Shoulders, and with a Fanatical Grin, which they use for a Smile, said, with a *Gusto*. The Q_____*n has a fine white Neck*, _______ What he might insinuate by it, is a Horror to me to imagine, wherefore I shall leave it to those that are in Authority, to be explain'd.

Another very eminent Man, of very great Distinction in the City of *London* for Riches, Atheism, and Immorality, being in a publick Coffee-House, I will not say whether *Garraway*'s or *Jonathan*'s, but it was one of them, hearing some Gentlemen on that Day exclaiming against the barbarous Action that gave Being to the Anniversary, and holding an Argument of Kings being accountable to

God only, was pleas'd to interpose, by thrusting his Horns into Company, and saying, *He that held it in the Affirmative, was in the Right, which was a sufficient Reason for the Parliament of* England *to cut off King* Charles *the First's Head; and justified the Action, since in so doing, they sent him to God to make up bis Accounts with him.*

The time would fail me to enumerate the many Villanous Passages that have occurr'd on this deplorable Subject: Wherefore I shall conclude with this Remark, That they not only repeat this horrid Martyrdom in their Festivals every 30th of January, but the chief of their Teachers, who goes for an Apostle with them, St. *Baxter*, (who bragg'd, that *He had spent a Gallon of his Blood, fighting against the King*) in his *Saints Everlasting Rest,* Edit. 1649. p. 82, 83. affirms those of the Regicides, and other Rebels, who were then dead, went streight into Heaven, and names several of them, as *Brook*, *Pym*, *Hambden*, and *White*, who was one of the Regicides; and *Twiss*, who was Moderator of their Assembly of Divines, &c. and describes Heaven in the Form of a Parliament, and calls it *Parliamentum Beatum*. And we must suppose he meant it that Form of a Parliament they had *then*, that is, without a *King*. Which minds me of the Note in one of their Sermons, wherein they found Fault with our Translation of the *Bible*, (as made by Bishops) for that it was full of the *Kingdom of God*, and the *Kingdom of God*, over and over again, every where; but there was not a Word of the Parliament of God; which they hop'd to find in the Original.

But we are not to answer for what our Forefathers did, say the Religious *Review*, *Observator*, and the rest of our Whig Papers, *they are dead, and the Guilt lies at their Door*: Not remembring that such Offences are to be punish'd to the third and fourth Generation. Besides, what one single Person among the whole Fraternity of the Dissenters, that maintain the Principles of Forty One, as taking Arms against their Sovereign, &c. can be excepted from the Guilt of this execrable Murder? What one of them does not justify the Forty One Principle of *Power in the People*, and to *coerce their Kings*. It was this! this! which cut off the King's Head. It was not the *Ax*, but the *Hand* that struck with it: It was not the *Hand*, but those who *impower'd* him: It was not those who *impowr'd* him, but the *Principle* which possessed them, that was the *Original* and *Formal Executioner*. And whoever hold the same *Principle*, must be ready for the same *Work* again, if they will be *true* to themselves. They cannot say, that King *Charles* the First did suffer unjustly, because he deny'd the *Jurisdiction* of the Court, and refus'd to plead. He would not own the *Sovereign Authority of the People*, which was the *highest Treason*, if the Principles of Forty One be true. And he deserv'd to die like a Criminal, that stood mute, whether he was guilty of the particular Facts charged upon him or not. And whoever hold these Principles, are *Calf's-*

Head-Men, whether they go to their Feasts or not. So much for a Subject which all Christian Nations ought to be asham'd of, especially this, that makes so many Pretences of excel ling our Neighbours in Piety, when there is not one that has come up to us in the superlative Wickedness of putting our lawful Prince to death, and afterwards glory in an Action that calls for the Hatred of God and Man.

him, with what dexterity she could, into Sots-Paradise, the Bed: After which, like a prudent Woman, according to the Custom of good Hussives, she began to search his Pockets, for the remaining Pence, which, in his Drunken Sleeps, the always secur'd to herself as a lawful Perquisite; but it happen'd, after she had lugg'd out a few, Farthings, and his Thimble, the common Stock of a Town-Sempstress, upon further Enquiry, she found, in his Fob, two or three small Papers, which, by prying into, she discover'd to be Tickets of Invitation to the *Calf's-Head-Feast*, including Directions where it was to be held, and over the Printed Words, the Figure of an Ax, very handsomly Engraven; and at the Bottom, written, in a fair Hand, *The Victuals given gratis; nothing to be paid for besides Drink.* Which she had no sooner read, but *Efaith*, quoth the Goslip, *if the Devil stand at the Door, now I know where you meet, I'll be one among ye*. Accordingly, assumes one of the Tickets to her self, and returns the rest, also the Far things, to avoid Suspicion, from whence she had taken 'em; so continu'd very free and easy with her Husband, till the Festival-Day appear'd, as if she had quite forgot it. Her 'Spouse, in the Interim, having deliver'd out those Tickets he was to dispose of to his Friends, supplying the Defect of that which he had lost, as he verily thought, by his own Carelesness: And when the time came that his Attendance was requir'd at their Diabolical Meeting, notwithstanding the Protestations he had made to his Wife, he shook the binding Fetters off his tender Conscience, and gave her the slip a little before Noon, as the desir'd and expected, happening, at the same Instant, to leave uppon his Shop-Board, an old Black Suit of the Reverend Doctor B____'s, sent over Night, to be new vamp'd, which the Termagant having an Eye on, thought the best Disguise she could possibly make choice of to pusue her Resolution in. Accordingly, she whips off her hussifly Weeds, and flips on the cloathing of pretended Righteousness upon the Smock of *Babylon*, and buttoning the Good Man's Britches over the Love-Trap of Iniquity, found the Spiritual Garment fitted her as well as if it had been originally made to cover the frail Flesh of her by whom it was now polluted: So combing down her own Rats-Tail-Hair about her Ears, which happen'd to prove of a puritannick length, and putting on her Husbands old Hat, and other suitable Accoutrements, away she march'd, pursuant to the Directions of her Ticket, to the Festival-House, which was in *Kings-street*, *Westminster*, where, upon Delivery of her Summons, the was kindly admitted, without Scruple or Suspicion of being a Cloven-Belly'd Spy. Where, after she had been handed to pay a Complement to the Axe, which was plac'd as a Trophy at the upper end of the Room, she was lovingly accosted with, *You're welcome Brother*, and invited to sit down at a large Table, among the rest of the Company, who were all seated, expecting every Minute the entrance of their Dinner; some chopping down their Knives upon their Plates, (as herself afterwards told the Story) to shew they had nothing but Decollation in their Thoughts; and others, in like manner, dividing their Bread into Mouthfuls, as if they were all practising to be expert Headsmen. Having by this time a little leisure to look round her, she espy'd her Husband, who could no more know her in her Fanatical Disguise, than a Man could a stol'n piece of Plate, which he had loft in the shape of a Tankard, and met with it in the form of a Candlestick.

At length in came the symbolical Eatables, as represented and explain'd in the beginning of this History: To which, as she reports, a lusty Greyheaded Holder forth, with one disconsolate Whisker on the sinister side of his Face, said a long cooling Grace, consisting of three Parts; first, he very distinctly curs'd all Kings and' Tyrants; secondly, pray'd heartily for all Saints and Regicides; and thirdly, crav'd a Blessing upon the Food and upon the Day, and then, like sociable Brother Rebels, they began to help themselves with all imaginable Alacrity: But the Botcher's Wife, ready to burst with Indignation when she see her forsworn Husband so very blythe and jocund, among so villanous a Crew, was unable longer to conceal her self or Passion (which cannot but be own'd as hard a Task for a Woman to dissemble, as for a Man to conquer) therefore resolving to postpone her Revenge no longer, just as her poor Spouse was lifting up his Hand with the first Mouthful to his Head, The snatch'd up a cloven Tongue, that,

The Westminster
Calf's Head Club

among many others, lay half bury'd in a Dish of Brains, and flung it in his Face with uncontroulable Fury, crying, at the fame Instant with an untunable Voice, *Remember your Oaths, you Rogue, will you damn yourself, you Dog, for a slice of Veal and Bacon.* The Taylor was so startled at the greasy Salutation, his Eyes blinded, and his Face so besmear'd with Sage and Brains, as if done on purpose to affront his Wit and Gravity, that he was quite confounded; which Assault was seconded by a Porringer of Green-sauce, that plaister'd his Countenance, and made the poor Devil look as if he had tumbl'd headlong into a Calf's Surreverence. *A Murrain take you for a confounded Witch, are you there! replies the snarling Sufferer, I know your Tongue, tho' you have disguis'd your Tail, and chang'd your Petticoats to be a worse Devil in Britches: But, Nouns, says he, since I must be hindered from eating of the Meat, I'll take care you shall be plentifully supply'd with the Sauce,* and then courageoully discharg'd such a handful of Brains in his Wife's Face, that put her almost in as bad a pickle as *Tom Thumb,* when he tumbl'd into the Pudding-Bowl. The Dame, in great Fury, returning the like Volley upon her grinning Adversary, crying, *Take that you Rogue, Sauce for the Goose is Sauce for the Gander.* The rest of the Company being as much a maz'd as if the Quarrel was design'd to betray them into the Hands of some approaching Magistrate, the King-killing Rebels sneaking down Stairs, one after another, for fear the growing Disturbance should occasion them, in the end, to be taken into Custody, or at least expose them to the Mercy of the Rabble, who, by reason of the Room being next the Street, were beginning to gather in a Crowd at the Door, and to put themselves upon Enquiry into what was the matter; so that at length none were left in the Room but the two Combatants and the Landlord, whom they brought in for a snack, for endeavouring to pacify the Difference; he not daring to interpose his Authority as Master of the House, because the ruine of his Family depended upon the Discovery; but was forc'd to use, for his own fake, the most soothing Means that possibly he could, to bring them into Temper with each other, without reflecting upon the Damage he had sustain'd by the Disappointment of his Company, but pleaded ignorance, made twenty Excuses, and with much difficulty reconcil'd the Adversaries: And when he had done, was glad to treat them with the best Liquors his House afforded, and to send them, when Maudlin, home in a Coach, that his extraordinary Civility might engage them to Secresy, which they both mutually promis'd; and were ever after so very honourable as not to discover the particular House.

Thus many Accidents, we find, often happen between the Cup and the Lip, which gives some Grounds for that extra vagant Saying, so frequently us'd by disappointed Persons, *viz* . *That a Man is sure of nothing, in this World, but what sticks in his Throat and will neither move up, nor down.* To conclude this Story, when the Botcher had furbish'd up the Doctor's old Suit, according to Direction, and carry'd it home, at the timeappointed, *Pray Doctor*, quoth the Botcher, *be not angry if I ask you one Question. What's that?* reply'd the Reverend Teacher. *Was you ever*, quoth Stitch, *at the* Calf's-Head Club? *No, Saucebox*, answer'd the Doctor, *Why ask you me that Question? Because, Sir*, quoth the Botcher, *if it were not you, I am sure I met the Devil there in your Cloaths. Then Sirrah*, reply'd the Doctor, *it is you that have dealt with him, and not I, or the Devil could never have been catch'd in my Coat; for I'd have you to know, I scorn so wicked a Knave should be found in my Sleeve.* After which, the Botcher, in excuse of his Jest, was forc'd to tell the Story to his attentive Guide, who, in spite of his dissembl'd Gravity, fell into a loud Laughter, and so they parted.

January 30. Annoq; Dom. 1709.

An eminent Bookseller, near *Leaden Hall*, forgetting the solemn Anniversary appointed for the Martyrdom, had bought, thro' Inadvertency, a Calf's-Head for his Family-Dinner upon that Day, and when the Bones were pick'd by his Servants, the Cook-Maid happen'd to toss'em into the Street before her Master's Door, with the like Innocence as he had sent in the same from Market; which unhappy Accident was greatly taken notice of by several Neighbours, who had an utter Abhorrence to the occasion of the Fast: insomuch that they reflected with no little Severity upon the Bookseller's Reputation: Among the rest, a Leatherseller in the Neighbourhood, who was a strict Loyalist, and a zealous Churchman, being inform'd of the Matter, reply'd, *I can scarce believe so fair a condition d Neighbour can be a Man of such wicked Principles as to make a Calf's-Head-Feast in bis own Family, upon a Day appointed for so Solemn a Fast*: Therefore, to satisfy himself in the Truth of the Report, step'd out of his own, to the Bookseller's, Shop-door, to behold the Testimonies of his Guilt, that lay expos'd in the Street; where, to his great Surprise, he found a Spaniel, which himself kept for his own Pleasure, very busy with the Scraps, *A Pox take your Chops for a Fanatical Puppy*, cries the Leatherseller to his Dog, *after all the expensive. Education I have given you, under Tim the Cobler, are you turn'd Regicide? Will nothing serve you, upon the Thirtieth of January, but a Calf's-Head for your Dinner*. Then rating off the Dog from his unseasonable Banquet, decoy'd him home, and in the height of his Indignation, condemn'd the poor Cur to be instantly hang'd, without Mercy, which occasion'd a Brother of the Quill to entertain his Friends with the following Elegy upon the unfortunate Offender.

Alas, poor Dog, 'twas very bard,
A Halter should dispatch thee hence;

Methinks one Puppy might have spar'd
    Another for the first Offence
Thou never read ft an Almanack,
    Or Proclamation, to be sure;
Therefore, for Ignoramus sake,
    Thy Fury should have sav'd the Cur.
In Man it would have been a Crime,
    But in a Dog 'twas no such thing;
Who knew not 'twas a fasting time,
    Or Malice bore to Queen or King.
Had not thy Master kept thee bare,
    Thoud'st not have know'd an empty Skull,
Nor didst thou know, I dare to swear,
    A Calf's-Head from a Napper's-Null.[1]
Therefore since Ign'rance was alone
    The fatal Cause of thy Mistake,
'Twas pity that so bare a Bone
    Should to the Halter bring thy Neck.
No *Cornish* Jury would have hang'd
    A Dog for such a Crime as thine.
I must confess I'd scarce have bang'd
    Thy Hide, bad'st been a Dog of mine.
So cruel no Man would have been,
    For such a Fault, I fancy rather,
Thy Master bang'd thee for thy Skin,
    Because bis Dealings are in Leather.
Tho' done in Anger or in Jest,
    Or owing to the hopes of Gain,
He's but a worse Calf's-Head, at best,
    Than that which brought thee to thy bane.

1 Cant for a Sheep's-Head.

Dr. Burgises Theater

The Whiggish Managers Prosecution of Doctor *Sacheverel*, provoking the Good People of *England* to show their Resentments, in pulling down the Meeting-Houses, upon the First of *March*, in the same Year, we have thought fit, in Memory of their notable Exploits, to introduce the preceeding Cut, being a lively Representation of the general Attack, which the enrag'd Rabble lo successfully made upon Doctor *Burgess*'s Theatre in *Rogue-Lane*, where the Gallows had the Honour to stand formerly, before *Tyburn* was erected.

For Bold Adventures, in so just a Cause,
Tho' done by Force, repugnant to the laws,
Deserve eternal Mem'ry and Applause.

January 30. 1710

A Widow Gentlewoman in the City of *Duresme*, alias *Durham*, who had the Misfortune to be hatch'd under a Potlid Hat and a Puritanical Cloak, 'till her sanctify'd Ladyship had unhappily imbib'd such Fanatical Principles as made her an absolute Virago in the defence of Schism, Faction, and Rebellion; in the encouragement of which she thought it no less than her in dispensable Duty, to spend her Annual Income was therefore glad and vigilant to shew her Zeal upon all Occasions, in reviving and promoting the *Good-Old-Cause*, that the same might be recover'd into the like Prosperity which the Saints enjoy'd before the Restoration, when they had founded *Dominion* in *Rebellion* and *Hypocrisy*, instead of *Grace*; and *Religion* in *Ignorance* and *Infidelity*, instead of *Faith* and the *Holy Scriptures*, the only Rule thereof. Among the rest of the Punctilio's in which she was over careful to manifest her Aversion to *Monarchy* and *Popery*, an Odium which the Party have always thrown upon the *Establish'd Church*. She was a strict and passionate Controller of the Anniversary Fast, which the Laws have set apart for King *Charles*'s. Martyrdom, providing always a *Calf's-Head-Feast* upon that Day, in her own House; to which bountiful Entertainment she was careful to invite all such Persons in the Town who were eminently rooted in Rebellious Principles. But to conclude her Tragedy, it happen'd upon the Day abovemention'd, that after she had eaten a very plentiful Dinner, in contempt of that unparallel'd Murder, which ought not to be thought of with out Horror and Amazement, she was suddenly struck by the Vengeance of Heaven, and drop'd down dead in the midst of her Jollity. Which was so merciful a Warning to the rest of the Regicides there present (for so we may justly term them, for their wicked Approbation of so impious a Fact) that they never durst meet after upon the like occasion in that City, left the terrible Displeasure of an avenging GOD should punish them for their Insolence in the like manner.

Upon the same Day an eminent Cook, near *Aldersgate*, who had been a frequent Encourager and

Entertainer of such sort of unjustifiable Meetings as aforemention'd, drop'd down dead at a *Calf's-Head-Feast* held in his own House, in the midst of their audacious Mirth, having not time enough allow'd him to ask GOD forgiveness for the contemptuous Wickedness he was unhappily engag'd in at the very moment of his Expiration.

On the Foregoing Judgments
A POEM

Since they who vainly call themselves the Saints,
Own God does all things to his Will bestow,
Why should they not believe the King that reigns
From Heav'n derives his Power here below?
And if they do, how durst they to attempt
The Sacred Person of the Prince that rules,
Both by the Laws of God and Man exempt
From the rude hands of daring Knaves and Fools?
Oh! touch not my Anointed, saith the Lord,
Obey the *Powers*, saith the Wise *S. Paul*,
How then can Rebels justify the Sword,
Or cursed Axe that wrought their Prince's fall?
Christians they cannot be, but rather shame
The Name of that Religion they profess,
And deviate from those Laws by which the

Same is here establish'd to our happiness.
How vile and wicked must those Wretches
be!
How much more impious their audacious
Guides,
Who teach'em to rebelliously agree
With Faction and infernal Regicides!
To solemnly approve and to commend
The most inhumane Act that i'er was done,
That the curs'd Guilt may flourish and de-
scend
From the dead Father on the living Son .
But sure such Instances of beav'nly Wrath,
As in these fad Examples have been show'd,
Must make the Rebel Brood forsake the Path
Their vile Progenitors so boldly trod.
But if they persevere in their defect,
And at their hellish Feasts in triumph meet,
May the all-powerful angry God correct.
Their stubborn Folly, as Himself thinks fit.

January 30. 1711

A certain Company of Fanaticks, who us'd to meet often at a precise Tavern at the upper-end of Cornwal, among whom were a couple of those stiffneck'd Puritans called *Quakers*, had agreed together to have a *Calf's-Head-Feast* upon the Day abovemention'd, at a Victuallers of their Acquaintance without *Bishops-Gate*, to who in they accordingly gave timely Orders for the Preparation of the Dinner; but when the Day came, and most of the Company were assembld at the House, one of the Quaking Puritans, who had promis'd to attend the Diabolical Solemnity, happend to be so affected with a Qualm of Conscience, that he thoughtless Iniquity to break his Word, than to be present at a Meeting that might endanger his Reputation, and prove an ugly detriment to his worldly Interest, which in all Cases is a prevailing Argument with those Money loving Saints. However, tho' he did not go according to his Promise, he was so civil as to send the following Epistle to his old Friends and Companions in excuse of his Omission. Thus superscrib'd:

To my Loving Friends, and in particular to him who is a Follower of the Light.

The Spirit, whom ye know beareth absolute Dominion over the Flesh, hath forbid me tasting of that carnal Food,which I verily suspect is banded in among ye upon this Day as a bloody Sacrifice. Aaron, *called the High-Priest in the dead Letter, concerning whom there is much written, when be tempted bis Followers to bow down and worship that Molton Image, which was framed like a Calf, tho' the wife Artificer caus'd the Idol to be made of masly Gold, that desired Mammon, which bumbleth the stiffnecked, and maketh the Humble Proud Lord was angry with his chosen People for worshipping the Beast, tho' it was formed of Gold, which commandeth all things, and was in great Wrath with the Sons of* Israel, *for turning from the Light to become Idolators. Therefore, my Friends, the Spirit moveth me to tell ye, upon this Red-Letter Day, that you are erred from the Light, in worshipping the Head of a Calf in the Flesh, whose Worth amounteth but to a few Pence, much more than the* Israelites *of old in falling down before the likeness of the same Creature, whose Head we may conceive to be of greater Value than a Herd of Oxen, or all the Calves in* Ascalon*: Therefore I cannot join with ye.*

The Letter of the Law, as well as the inward Man, forbiddeth me to be present at such Carnal Meetings, where ye only trample on the Neck of the dead Antichrist; but follow your fleshly Appetites, against the Convictions of the Light, and drown the Spirit of Truth in the Cups of Immoderation: Therefore I cannot join with ye.

It is also to be feared, that ye turn the Meekness which becometh the Saints, into Vials of Wrath, which your unbridl'd Tongues pour out without Mercy upon the Whore of Babylon and the Priests of Baal, till ye have lost that Patience and Moderation, which ought to arm the Elect against the Power of Sathan: Therefore I cannot join with ye; tho' I am to all Lovers and Followers of the Light a Friend in Sincerity.

Habbakuk Cowdry.

An Account of the Puppit-Plot, Intended to Have Been Put in Practice, on November the 17th 1711. Queen Elizabeth's Birth-Day

On *Friday* the Sixteenth of *November*, the Heads of the Party met at the New Palace, where the late *Viceroy* recounted to them the happy Disposition of Affairs, and concluded, *That notwithstanding all their Misfortunes, they had still to Morrow for it.* This Person, who has so often boasted himself upon his Talent for *Mischief, Invention, Lying*, and for making a certain *Lilli bullero Song*, with which, if you will believe himself, he sung a deluded Prince out of Three Kingdoms, was resolv'd to try if, by the Cry of *No Peace, High Church, Popery*, and the Pretender, he could Halloo another in. In order thereto several Figures were dress'd up, fifteen of which were found in an empty House in *Drury-lane*; the *Pope*, the *Pretender*, and the *Devil*, seated under a *State*, whereof the Canopy was Scarlet Stuff, trimmed with deep Silver Fringe; the *Pope* was as fine as a *Pope* need to be, the *Devil* as terrible, the *Pretender* habited in Scarlet laced with Silver, a full fair long Periwig, and a Hat and Feather. They had all white Gloves, not excepting the very Devils, which, whether quite so proper, I leave to the Learned. This *Machine* was designed to be born upon Men's Shoulders; the long Train dependant from the *Figures*, were to conceal those that carried them. Six *Devils* were to appear as drawing the Chariot, to be followed by four *Cardinals*, in fine proper Habits; four *Jesuits*, and four *Franciscan Friars*, each with a pair of white Gloves on, a pair of Beads, and a Flaming, or, if you please, a Bloody, Faulchion in their Hands. Pray judge, if such a Parade should at any time appear, without the proper Disposition of Lights, c. as was here intended, do you not believe it would be a sufficient Call to the Multitude? and that they would never forsake it ' till their Curiosity had been satisfied to the full? Any Man in his Senses may find this was a deliberate, as well as a great Expence, to prepare Men's Minds for Sedition. One *Stoughton*'s Sermon (which was lately burnt by the Common Hangman in Ireland, by Order of the House of Lords) Preached at St. Patrick's in Dublin, and Printed there, was that very Week Re-printed here, and handed about with extream Diligence: And to fill the People with false Fear and Terror, they had some Days before reported, that the Q____ was dangerously ill of the Gout in her Stomach and Bowels: The very Day of the designed Procession, it was whisper'd upon the *Exchange*, and over all the City, that She was Dead. A Gentlewoman that makes Wax-work, declares, that some time before, certain Persons of Quality, as she judged, who called one another Sir *Harry*, Sir *John*, Sir *James*, &c. came to her House, and be spoke several Wax-work Figures, one for a Lady; they agreed to her Price, paid half in Hand, and the rest when they fetch'd them away. These Figures are not yet taken. One was designed to represent the L__d T____r, the Lady Mrs. *Ma_____m*, and the rest the other great Officers of the Court, with Dr. *S_____l*; which the Work-woman was ordered to make as like his Picture as possibly the could. A certain Lady, renowned for Beauty, at the P_____ss's Palace, desired that she might have the Dressing up of the *Young, handsome Statesman*, whose bright Parts are so terrible to the Enemies of his Country; in order to it, she proposed borrowing from the Play-house, *Æsop's large white horse-hair Periwig*: Her L___d furnish'd out the rest of the Materials from the Q___'s *W_d_be*. No wonder he should be an Enemy to Peace, when his Father gains so much by the Continuance of the War. Nor that a certain young D____ was so eager to have him go in Disguise with the *Viceroy*, since it was agreed, upon the Husbands Absence, that the said Nobleman should *pass the Night* with his L____y.

Further, to convince you that this was e premeditated Design, and carried on in all its Forms, proper Persons had been busie before-hand to secure a thousand Mob to carry Lights at this goodly Procession: One of these Agents came to a Victualling-House in *Clare-Market*, he called for Drink, and the Master of the House, of whom he enquired if he could procure him forty stout Fellows to carry *Flambeauxs* on *Saturday* the 17th Instant, to meet there at one a Clock, they should have a Crown a piece in Hand, and whatever they drank till five, he would be there to see discharged. At such a Proposal, mine Host prickt up his Ears, and told the Managers, his Honour need not fear but that he might have as many as his Honour pleased at that Price: Accordingly he fetched in several from the Market, *Butchers, Tripe-men, Poulterers' Prentices*, who joyfully listed themselves against the Day, because it was to be a Holy-day, and they should not stand in need of their Masters leave, for on Q____ *Bess*'s Day, they said, they always went out of course. The Landlord promised to make up the Complement by the appointed Time, with honest Lads, who would be glad to get their Bellies full of Drink, and a Crown a piece in an honest way. All was agreed upon, the Gentleman paid the Reckoning, which came to a considerable Sum in Beer and Brandy for his Mob, and departed, with assurance of being there at One a Clock to meet his *Mirmidons*; but the Matter being discovered, he has not been heard of since, to the great Disappointment of the good Man, and the People he had engaged. The like was done in several other parts of the Town. They had secured to the number, as I told you, of One Thousand Persons, who were so hired to carry Lights, tho' they knew, not to what End, doubtless for a *Burial*, among whom were many of the very Foot-Guards. Drinking from One to Five, 'tis plain they were to be made Drunk, the better to qualify them for what Mischief was designed by their proper Leaders. The *Viceroy*, with some others of as good, and two or three of better Rank than himself, were resolved to act in disguise; the *Viceroy* like a *Seaman*, in which he hoped to out-do *Massanello* of *Naples*, whose Fame he very much envies for the mighty Mischief he occasioned: His busie Head was the first Inventor of the Design, and he would take it very ill if he were robbed of the Glory He had lately proved the Power of an *accidental Mob*, and therefore hoped much better from a *premeditated One*: He did not doubt inflaming them to his Wish, by the Noise of *Popery* and the *Pretender*, by which they would be put into a Humour to burn even Dr. S. and the other *Effigies*. At their several Bonefires, where the *Parade* was to make a Stand, the Preliminary Articles were to be thrown in, with a Cry of, *No Peace*, and proper Messengers were to come Galloping, as if like to break their Necks, their Horses all in a Foam, who should cry out, *The Q____, the Q____ was dead* at Hampton-Court At the same time the D_____ of *M_____* was to make his Entry thro' *Aldgate*, where he was to be met with the Cry of, *Victory, Bouchain, the Lines, no Peace, no Peace*. If Matters had once come to this pass, I do not see what could have hindred the Leaders from doing all the Mischief they desired, from exalting and pulling down whom they pleased, nor from executing, during the Rage of the People, prepossessed, as they would be, with the News of the Q____'s Death, whatever Violence, Injustice and Cruelty, they should think fit. They had resolved before, what Houses should be burnt: They were to begin with one in *Essex-street*, where the Commissioners of Accompts meet; from whence a late Discovery has been made of vast Sums annually received by a great Man, for his Permission to serve the Army with Bread. They said, *H______y* should have better Luck than they expected, if he escaped *De Witting*;[2] they would set People to watch him all that Day, that they might know whereto find him when they had occasion. And truly, who can answer for the Consequence of such a Tumult, the Rage of a mad drunken Populace, fomented by such Incendiaries, (for the whole Party, to a Man, were ingaged to be there) I don't see how the City could have escaped Destruction?

But I cannot but look up to *God Almighty* with Praise for our Deliverance, and really think we have very much need of a Thanksgiving, for in all probability the Mischief had been universal and *irremediable*. I tremble to think what lengths they would have gone: I dare not so much as imagine it. They had taken *Massanello*'s Insurrection[3] for a Precedent, by which all who were not directly of their own Party had suffered, as may be gathered from what we know of their Nature, and by what is

2 *See* Charles Leslie's *Gallienus Redivivus, or Murther will out, &c. Being a true Account of the De Witting of Glencoe, Gaffney* (Edinburgh, 1695). —Ed.

3 Italian fisherman, Tommaso Aniello, abbreviated Masaniello (1620 – 1647), led a revolt in 1647 against the rule of Habsburg Spain in the Kingdom of Naples. —Ed.

already discovered, tho' there is doubtless a great deal more behind. As soon as the Figures were seized, they dispatched a Messenger Express to the Place where it was known the D_____ intended to Land, to tell him he might now take his own Time, there was no occasion *for his being on the seventeenth Instant, by seven at Night*, at Aldgate; and so he lay that Night five Miles short of the Town.

However the *Viceroy* may value himself upon this Design, he seems but to have copied my Lord *Sh____y*[4] in 1679, on the same Anniversary. It is well known, by the Favour of the Mob, they hoped then to have made the Duke of *Monmouth* King,[5] who was planted at Sir *Thomas Fowls*'s at Temple-Bar, to wait the Event; whilst the rest of the great Men of his Party, were over the way at Henry the Eighth's Taverti. King *Charles* had been persuaded to come to Sir *Francis Child*'s to see the Procession,

4 Even though he opposed James' succession to Charles II on account of the former's Catholicism and similarities with French absolutism, Anthony Ashley Cooper, 1st Earl of Shaftesbury PC FRS (1621 - 1683) had been funded and supported by Louis XIV, since it was in the latter's interest to deepen divisions in England. However, in 1681, Louis XIV switched support to Charles. —Ed.

5 James Scott, 1st Duke of Monmouth (1649 - 1685) led a rebellion designed to depose Charles II's successor, James II. Two years earlier, although in exhile in the Netherlands, he had been a co-conspirator in the Rye House Plot, which aimed at assassinating Charles II and his son James, then Duke of York. And this in turn came on the back of a 1681 Parliamentary effort to exclude James from succession, a manoeuvre thwarted by Charles when he dissolved the Oxford Parliament. —Ed.

but before it began, he had private Notice given him to retire, for fear of what Mischief the *Mob* might be wrought up to: He did so, which ruined the Design they had to seize on his Person, and proclaim the Duke, King. This was the Scheme our *Modern* Politicians went upon. One of them was heard to say, *They must have more Diversions than one, i.e. burning, for the good People of London, since the Mob loved to Create,*[6] *as well as Destroy*.

By this time, I do not doubt, but all Men are throughly convinced of the Innocence of this intended Procession, which they publickly avow, and tell the M____y they are welcome to make what they can of it, knowing themselves safe by having only intended, not acted the *Mischief*; if it had once come to *That*, they would have been so far above the fear of Punishment for their own Crimes, as to become Executioners of the Innocent.

Truly, I think the *Malice* of that Party is Immortal, since not to be satiated with twenty three Years Plunder, the Blood of so many Wretches, nor the Immense Debt with which they have burthened us.

Through the unexampled Goodness of the Q____, and the lenity of the other Parts of the *Legislature*, they are suffered to sit down unmolested, to bask and revel in that Wealth they have so unjustly acquired; yet they pursue their Principles with unwearied Industry, club their *Wit*, *Money*, *Politicks*, towards restoring their Party to that Power from whence they are fallen; which, since

6 Make a K__g.

they find so difficult, they take care, by all Methods, to disturb and vilify those who are in Possession of it. *Peace* is such a bitter Pill they know not how to swallow: To poyson the People against it, they turn, they try every Nail, and have at last hit of one they think will go, and that they drive to the Head: They cry, *No Peace*, 'till the Trade of our own Nation be entirely given up to our Neighbours. Thus they would carry on the Publick Good of *Europe*, at the Expence of our Private Destruction. They cry our *Trade* will be ruin'd if the *Spanish West-Indies* remain to a Son of *France*. Tho' the Death of his Father may cause *Philip* to forget his Birth and Country which he left so Young. After the Decease of his Grandfather, he will be, *only* the *Brother* of a haughty rough-natured King, who, in all probability, may give him many Occasions to become every Day more and more a *Spaniard*.

They do not allow the *Dauphin*'s or the *Emperor*'s Death[7] have made an Alteration in Affairs, and confide all things to the supine Temper of the *Austrian* Princes, from whence they conclude there can be no Danger in trusting half *Europe* to the easy unactive Hands of such an Emperor. But may not another *Charles* the Fifth arise? Another *Philip* the Second? Who, tho' not possessed of the *Austrian* Territories, gave more Trouble and Ter-

7 Louis, Dauphin of France, known as the Grand Dauphin (b. 1661) eldest son of Louis XIV and Maria Teresa of Spain, died on 14 April 1711, while Joseph I (b. 1678), Holy Roman Emperor, died on 17 April 1711. —Ed.

ror to *England*, than ever the felt from *France*; insomuch, as had not the Seas and Winds fought our Battles, their *Invinceable Armada* had certainly brought upon us Slavery, and a Popish Queen. Neither is it a new Thing for Princes to *Improve* as well as *Degenerate*. Power generally brings a Change of Temper. *Philip de Comines* tells us, That the Great Duke of *Burgundy*[8] in his Youth hated the Thoughts of War, and the Fatigue of the Field. After he had fought and gained could never be easy in Peace, but led all his Life in War, and at length died in it; for want of other Enemies, fighting against the poor barren *Swissers*, who were possessed of nothing worth contending for.

But it is not *Reason*, or even *Facts*, that can subdue this *Stubborn* Party; they bear down all by Noise and Misrepresentation; they are, but will not seem convinced, and make it their Business to pre vent others from being so. If they can but Rail and raise a Clamour, they hope to be believed, though the miserable Effects of their *Male-administration* are Ten thousand to One against them. A festering obvious Sore, which when it can be healed we know not, though the most famous Artists apply their constant Skill to endeavour at a Cure. Their Aversion to any Government but their own, is unalterable; like some *Rivers*, that are said to pass through without mingling with the Sea, tho' disappearing for a time, they arise the same, and never change their Nature.

8 Charles the Bold, Duke of Burgundy (1433 - 1477). —Ed.

January 30. 1712

The Fanatical Saints being highly exasperated at the great Disappointment the Reverend Dr. *Sacheverel* gave upon his Tryal, to the over-hasty Managers, those invenom'd Tygers of the impatient Faction, were resolv'd to let slip no opportunity of shewing their Resentments, and of spitting their Malice at the Church and Government, especially upon that Day which hath been set apart by the Wisdom of Parliament, for the Kingdom to atone, in the most solemn manner, for the past Evils of a wicked Generation; so that as a further Specimen of their daring Presumption, I shall entertain the Reader with the following Story, as it was trans acted in *Southwark*, by some angry Zealots, upon the Day premis'd.

The 26th of *January*, in the Year above mention'd, proving a Market-Day in the Borough of *Southwark*, some of the Country Imposers upon Ignorance and Necessity, had brought a Carrionly Slink, or at least a Rainbow colour'd Calf, shrewdly suspected to die of a Consumption, into the Publick Market; which, in all probability, was contriv'd on purpose to give the angry Saints a seasonable opportunity of shewing their contempt of the solemn Anniversary appointed for the Martyrdom of King Charles the First: For the two Persons, nam'd *Moses Web* and *John Gun*, whose bus'ness it was to overlook the Market, under the Title of *Flesh-Tasters*, being both rigid Dissenters, and Men whose tender Consciences were full of many scrupulosities against Church, Queen, and Government; also zealously bent to the utter destruction of Doctor *Sacheverel*, for the singular Service he had done his native Country in the Times of Danger, to the apparent hazard of his own Happiness: I say, those two Fanaticks, in a survey of the Market, according to their Duty, finding the Calf aforemention'd to be perfect Carrion, and fit for nothing, at best, but to make Pottage *Alamode* for a necessitous Family of *French Protestants*, thought proper to seize the same, pretendingly to burn it, according to the Statute in that Case provided, which they ought to have done upon the same Day, in the publick Market; but the better to answer their malicious Ends, they vouchsaf'd to postpone the Execution thereof till the *Thirtieth of January*, and then ordering a Bonfire on St. *Margaret's-Hill*, did, in open contempt of the Murder of King *Charles*, as well as in derision of the solemn Fast upon that Occasion, burn the Head and Neck, apart from the Body, in a riotous manner; which audacious Proceeding being taken notice of by some of the Neighbours, who were Persons of too much Humanity to behold so detestable an Act without discovery, particularly Three, whose Names were *Robert Marshal*, *William Rubidge*, and *Thomas Havergil*; and these, as became their Duty, inform'd against the Offenders, upon Oath, and caus'd them to be summon'd before *John Lade*, *Walter Cook*, and *William Overman*, Esquires, Three of Her Majesty's Justices of the Peace for the County of *Surrey*, before whom they were plainly Convicted, not only by undeniable Evidence, but by their own Confession, having little to alledge in their Defence, but that they did it in pursuance of the Statute, and that the other Joints were burnt along with the Head; which did not appear by the Evidence to be truth, who depos'd, they saw no other Part, but the Head and Neck, which they took out of the Fire. And as a further Testimony of the ill meaning had couch'd under the Execution of their Office, which specious pretence they thought sufficient to have skreen'd them from ensuing Trouble, one *William Stevens*, of the Borough, depos'd upon Oath, That when the said *Web* was disswaded from burning the Carrion upon so improper a Day, his Answer was, *That be would roast the Head for Doctor Sacheverel's Supper*: Which is a plain Indication, that the same was intended in derision of the Fast, and could not be done unthinkingly, after such a Precaution. So that the Transgressors were bound over to answer their Offence at the next Quarter-Sessions, where they were both Convicted of Misdemeanor by the former Evidence; tho' the Mercy of the Court was such, that the Two Brothers in Iniquity were only find Twenty Marks each, and to lie in Goal till the Money was paid, and they had given in Sureties for their Good-Behaviour. Thus, in such notorious Instances as these, we may not only annually, but daily observe, in one Case or other, the flagrant Malice and in sufferable Impudence of such Fanatical Incendiaries as glory in the barbarous Treasons of their Forefathers, and are impatiently covetous of Opportunities to perpetrate the like daring Villanies; for whoever are so far corrupted in their Principles as to zealously approve of the most impious Act that ever was attempted by the Sons of Satan in the disguise of Sanctity, have nothing to reclaim their violent Natures from immoderately lusting after the fame Wickedness; and would, if they could, by a frequent Repetition of the like Cruelties, make Rebellion, Murder, and the worst Enormities, lawful in any sanctify'd Desperado, by dint of Custom.

Who therefore that has Sence and Gratitude enough to consider the Welfare and Security of their own native Country, and the Honour and Safety of those who have a Right to Rule us, can blame Them, in the midst of Danger, for inclosing the Government from those Factious Trespassers who seek Authority, to turn it against the Church and State, from whence they derive the same; and only covet to be near the Throne, that they may the better undermine it; for nothing can endanger the *British* Constitution but the Treachery of Persons entrusted in the State, who are Enemies to the Government; and the Infidelity and Hypocrisy of *Geneva* Wolves, crept into Sheeps Cloathing; as is well observ'd by an Ingenious Gentleman in the following Verses.

O *Britain!* they're not open Foes
That Thou hast cause to dread;
Pretended Friends, alas, are those
By whom thou'st been betray'd.
Such as fate high in Church and State,
Who aw'd the little Knaves
And Fools that rais'd'em to be Great,
That they might make us Slaves.
France, the Pretender, and the Pope,
The Faction bid us fear,
Whilst they advance Designs, in hope
To gain Dominion here.
And if we take not timely Care
To guard the Church and Crown,
The Saints, who with such Heat declare
For War, will pull'em down.
They'll tack-about with all their Hearts,
And swear to be our Friends,
But trusted, act their wonted Parts,
To gain their wicked Ends.
If therefore they're restor'd to Pow'r,
We do the Work by halves,
And let loose Tygers to devour
Ourselves like silly Calves.
Besides, 'twill look as if we fear'd
To split on Factious Shelves,
Or that the Course our Friends have steer'd
Was but to serve themselves.
'Tis therefore best to muzzle those
That growl so much at home;

For Kings that fawn upon their Foes
Are eas'ly overcome.

Besides the Pains which are annually taken by our Republican Saints and Regicides, upon the *Thirtieth of January*, in open contempt of the most execrable Treason that ever was perpetrated in a Christian Country; since the notorious Proceedings against Dr. *Sacheverel*, which exasperated their old Friends the Rabble, to shew themselves such Enemies to the aspiring Faction, they have been equally diligent upon all other Occasions, to affront the Government by their Riotous Festivals and Meetings, in order to recover their lost Instruments, the Mob, into their Factious Power, without whose Assistance they are totally unable to raise such Commotions and Disturbances as they have the Folly to think would give new Life and Encouragement to those fading Plots and Machinations by which the credulous Saints hope, at one time or other, to make themselves Masters of the promis'd Land, tho' at present they are driven back from the fight thereof, into the wide Wilderness. We therefore think it but a pardonable Digression from the Design in hand, to introduce the several riotous Attempts the disgusted Faction have industriously made, in the present Year, to reconcile their old Friends the Rabble to a good Opinion of that declining Party, who have so long been seeking the destruction of the Kingdom, and are still buoy'd up with the Vanity to believe, that by the friendly Assistance of the Good People of *England*, (a flattering Title they have always confer'd upon Captain *Tom* and his Followers), that they might still compleat the Work of Rebellion, to the happiness of such Saints and Regicides who desire to prosper by a National Confusion.

After the Seizure of their Puppits in Drury. Lane, which put the Plotting Leaders of the angry Faction to so great a Disappointment, several Desperadoes of the Party took upon 'em the Name of *Mohocks* (from the Four Kings that came over from the *West-Indies*), and, under that Name, in the height of their Provocation, fell to practising the most unspeakable Barbarities in the publick Streets, that ever were heard of among Christians, Snickersneeing Passengers as they walk'd about their Business after Candlelight, with sharp Penknives, Razors, and other keen Instruments they had provided for their mischievous Attempts; stabbing People in the Arms, slitting of Noses, cut ting off Ears, pinking of Skins, tearing Women's Scarves, cutting down their Stays, scarifying their Shoulders, assaulting Constables and the Watch, striking such a Terror to the whole Town, by the Riots and Mutinies which they repeated nightly for some time, that People were fearful to pass the Streets after Daylight was shut in, left they should fall into the hands of these unaccountable Ruffians; till, at length, their Leader, whom the rest call'd their Emperour, in assaulting a Lady: passing homewards in a Chair, was so handsomely engag'd by the Chairmen with their Poles, that he receiv'd a Fracture in his Skull, which prov'd his Bane, tho' it was given out, being a Great Person, that he dy'd of the *Small-Pox*: Upon which Her Majesty was pleas'd to Issue out Her Royal Proclamation, wherein a Reward of Forty Pounds was promis'd to any Person who should Apprehend and Convict any of the said *Mohocks*, who were the wicked Actors in these insufferable Disturbances, which, in all probability, were carry'd on with a Factious Design of raising such Commotions, as might have been dangerous to the present Ministry, had not the Death of their Emperour, and the Wisdom of the State put a stop to their Barbarities.

The next signal Instance of the restless Temper of the revengeful Whigs and Regicides, was on the beginning of *October*, the Nativity of the Princess *Sophia*,[9] upon which Day a certain Whiggish Peer, noted for his Disaffection to the Queen and Government, join'd with a *Scotch* Lord, and other Persons of Distinction, most zealous Advocates for the same Party, assembl'd themselves in a Body at the *Bouffler's-Head* Tavern in *Southampton-street* near *Bloomsbury*-Market, where they order'd a great Bonfire to be kindled in the Evening, and plenty of strong Drink for the Entertainment of the Rabble, in hopes thereby to have tempted them to declare for the Low Church Interest and the *Han-*

9 Sophia of Hanover (1630 - 1714), the granddaugter of James I and VI, was heiress presumptive to the thrones of England and Scotland and Ireland under the Act of Settlement 1701. —Ed.

over Succession, without regard to the Church, Queen, and present Ministry. But the Mob finding, by their Whiggish Healths, the drift of their Deligo, call'd, *One and all*, with an audible Voice, to their noble Benefactors above Stairs, and desir'd they would begin a Health to the Church and Queen: Which they refusing to do, and drinking, instead of the Mob's Toast, *Confusion to the High-Church and Doctor Sacheverel*: So provok'd the Gentry of the Lower Classes, that snatching up Fire-Brands from the flaming Pile, they bombarded the House with such Unanimous Resolution, that in a few Minutes 'twas as hard a Matter to see a whole Pain of Glass in any of the Windows, within their reach, as to find an honest Serjeant at the Counter-Gate, or a forgiving Christian among the Whiggish Party; so that the Nobility were so baffl'd and disappointed by the Mobility, that they were force to withdraw from their House of Rendezvous, under great Dissatisfaction, to think the Mob were grown too cunning to sell their Interest in the Kingdom to a devouring Party, for a Barrel of strong Bub, and a Factious Bonfire, especially when they found they were so industriously fish'd for by a *Scotch* Anglers.

And to the Throne the greater tease.
Rais'd the whole Tribe to such a pitch
Of daring Pride and Insolence,
That they began to think, when Rich,
Rebellion could be no Offence.
And bad they not been timely cast
In Anger, from around the Throne,
They would have Bully'd, 'til at last
They'd made the Regal Power their own.
So the Rich Miser, who hath lent
A Mortgage Sue for sake of great
Extortion, never is content,
Till he's ingross'd the whole Estate.

The Malice of the expiring Faction, in belching out their Venom to the last Gasp, is remarkable in the two following Libels, set up publickly at *Kingston* upon *Thames*, one under Her Majesty's Statue, on the 30th of *January* last. The Title and Verses thus:

The Presbyterian Grace

May the Calves Heads which we have lately tasted,
Revive the Cause for which the Fools have fasted;
And may we thus commemorate this Day,
Till we have no more need to fast or pray.
Bless'd be those Saints, for ever bless'd be

those That murder'd *CHARLES*, and
every King depose.
Bless'd, O! For ever blessed be those Men
That give the next great Stroke, Amen,
Amen.

Set up in a different Place

Disgrac'd, undone, and made the Nation's
Sport,
From Places turn'd, and banish'd from the
Court,
Why did we not, Fools as we were, foresee
Our swift Destruction in a Monarchy:
Some Madness seiz'd us, sure, or we'd have
seen
Our certain Ruin in an *English Q____*:
For Fire with Water sooner can unite,
Than we can own Hereditary Right.

The Magistrates of the said Town, to express their Indignation against such horrid Provocations, did immediately make search, with Promise of Reward, for Discovery of the Incendiaries.

November 4. 1712

About ten Days before the Festival appointed for King *William*'s Birth, Mr. *W____house*, an eminent Merchant in the City of *London*, accompany'd with one *D_____son*, a Buttonmaker, went to the House of Mr. *Johnson*, Master of the *Three-Tuns* and *Rummer* Tavern in *Gracechurch-street*, and agreed with the said *Johnson* for the use of a large Room up one pair of Stairs, fronting the Street, upon the fourth of *November*; telling him, some Gentlemen desir'd to meet there at the time aforemention'd, to celebrate the Memory of the late King *William* over a Bottle and a Bonfire: To which Mr. *Johnson* very readily consented, but entertaining an Apprehension that so publick a Rejoicing might cause a Tumult at the Door, made a prudent Bar gain, that Mr. *W____house* should repair whatever Damage should be done to his House or Windows upon that Account. Which reasonable Article was willingly comply'd with, and so they parted.

On *Monday* the third of the same Instant Mr. *W____house* came again to Mr. *Johnson*'s House, and gave Orders for five Dozen Bottles of Wine to be ready drawn against the next Day, for the Gentlemen who were to meet in the Room appointed; and two Barrels of intoxicating Belch that might enliven the Mob, and encourage them to dance to a Whiggish Tune, when the Managers in the Balcony, should turn their Throats into Rebellious Bagpipes.

Also order'd him to prepare a plentiful number of Faggots, sufficient to erect a good Protestant Bon-fire, worthy of the Occasion. All which was punctually observ'd against the time appointed.

On the following *Tuesday*, being the Day of Solemnity, the Company assembl'd in the Evening, and Orders were dispatch'd to their Engineer to give Factious Fire to their Seditious Beacon, that the Mob might be allarm'd, and drawn into a Body by the flaming Pyramid. The Gentry Above Stairs, or the Upper-House of Mob, consisted, as reported, of near Two hundred; in which Convention of Whigs were four frightful Scaramouches, whose Faces were disguis'd with Theatrical Whiskers, their Hair or Perukes dock'd into the puritanical Crop, their Bodies truss'd up in short antiquated Jackets, such as worn by the Ruffians who attended the Martyrdom of King *Charles* the First; as if the Masqueraders, could they have brought over the Mob, were to have led their Followers into some desperate Assassination, to have gratify'd the Revenge of the fallen Party, upon some of the present Ministry: And the better to encourage whatsoever wicked Designs they had in hand, upon that riotous Meeting, it is credibly reported, that a certain Lord, since kill'd in a Duel, and another Peer, who not long before had at tempted to hang himself, with a Colonel of the Guards, and some other Whiggish Quality, were present in the Assembly; and that they were the Persons who appeard in the Balcony with their Swords animate the Mob to be-

gin Mischief, when drawn, which they brandish'd, in order to by their guzling Draughts they had intoxicated their Senses. The Balconians beginning a Health to the Queen and the House of *Hanover*, and follow'd the same with, *Success to the Low-Church and Confusion to the High*; which extravagant Excursion sate not easy upon the Stomachs of the Rabble, that they utterly refus'd to pledge their Benefactors, and were so incens'd, that the majority of the Mob, in direct opposition to the Whigs unchristian Wishes, cry'd, *God bless the High-Church and Doctor Sacheverel*; then pulling down the Pile, so bombarded the Balcony with Faggot Bats and Firebrands, that the worsted Enemy were glad to retire into close Quarters. After which the Assailants attack'd the Windows with such impracticable Fury, as if they had all been Glasiers.

The Tumult arising to such ungovernable Madness, that it was not in the Power of the Constables and Watch to suppress the Riot, but they were forc'd to send for the Trainbands of the City, who were out that Night to prevent Disorders; by whose Temper and Conduct, after great Difficulty, the Rabble were appeas'd. But this not answering the End of the Company who were congregated in the Tavern, the most desperate of the Cabal appear'd again in the Balcony, after the manner as before, assaulting the Constables and Trainbands with Billets and empty Bottles, those ugly Granadoes, till, among other Mischiefs, they unhappily wounded a Midnight-Magistrate. But not content with this

Success, the Noble Colonel of the Factious Party, to distinguish his Valour above the rest of his Associates, went down into the Street, and wrested a Truncheon out of a Marshal's Hand, as if he was, desirous to become their General; but the Trainband Officers, by their prudent management dispers'd the Mob, and put an end to the Disorders. The famous Governour *Johnson,*whose Castle of Clarret had suffer'd great. Damage in the fiery Storm, to make him part of amends was the next Day sent for by my Lord Mayor, by whom he was required to give a just Account of the over-nights Proceedings, but like a trusty *Trojan*, he refus'd, upon his Examination, to discover any Person present in the Riot, except Mr. *W____house*, who was also sent for, but deny'd Attendance without his Lordship's Warrant, which, pursuant to his own Stubbornness, was dispatch'd accordingly, and, by Vertue thereof, he was brought to be Examin'd, but, to shew his Integrity to the Faction, would discover nothing; affirming, *If the Same was to be done again, he would do it.* So that, in the Conclusion, they were both bound over to appear the next Sesssions, that their stiffneckedness might be humbled.

As a further Argument, to prove that the revengeful Faction had some desperate Design in hand, which they hop'd to have effected by this Riotous Meeting, in case they could have won the Rabble to have been of their Party; they had also put on foot, an infamous Contrivance, on the same Morning, in hopes thereby to compass the Destruction of the Lord-High Treasurer, the Truth of which is affirm'd to be as followeth.

On *Tuesday* Morning the 4th of *November*, the Penny-Post-Man deliver'd a Parcel at the Lord-Treasurer's House, directed to his Lordship's Porter, who, upon opening the same, found an enclos'd Box superscrib'd to his Lord, to whom the same was carry'd, as he was dressing in his Bed-Chamber, and receiv'd by his Lordship, who straining up the Lid, as far as the Packthread that ty'd it would give way, was surpriz'd with the sight of a Pocket Pistol, (as himself declar'd to a Gentleman of the Clergy then attending)[10] upon which, the Doctor desir'd leave to examine the Box at a distance from his Lordship, urging, *That a Pistol could be no less than a palpable Indication of some perrilous Contrivance.* Whereupon his Lordship deliver'd it to the Doctor, who took it to the Window, and pulling out his Penknife, cut, the Packthreads that bound the Box, to which were fasten'd some other Strings that govern'd the Implements within, which he also cut with all imaginable Caution, and then lifting up the Lid with Care and Leisure, for his own Security, beheld, to his great Amusement, a Pocket-Pistol, lying cross the middle of the Box, and fasten'd at each End with two Nails; on each side the Firelock, were laid the middle pieces of two large Inkhorns, charg'd with Powder and Ball, and Touch-holes bor'd at the Butt-ends thereof; to which were tied two Linen-Bags

10 Jonathan Swift. —Ed.

of Gunpowder, and at the Ends of the Bags, two Quills of Wild Fire, as appear'd afterwards upon a narrower Inspection; the Muzzles of the Ink-horn-Barrels were plac'd different ways, and one of the Quills directed to the Pan of the Pistol, as the other probably did before disorder'd by the Carriage. The Gentleman who open'd the Box, being some what startled. at so mischievous an Appearance, would not venture to touch the Pistol 'till he had carefully remov'd all the other Machines, then gently raising up the Lid still wider by degrees, found the Nails gave way by which the Stock of the Pistol was fasten'd at both Ends, whose Firelock, upon Examination, was ready prim'd and cocked, and a String fasten'd to the Trigger thereof, which the Examiner conceiv'd he had the fortune to cut in the first opening, which, had he escap'd, would, in all probability, have discharg'd the Pistol, whose Pan had Communication with the Bags of Powder, which, by blowing up, must have fired the Barrels that pointed different ways, so that the wicked Contrivance could scarce have fail'd of the intended Execution.

But the barbarous Design being thus happily prevented, the Projecters thereof, to secure their Party from the odious Reflection that must inevitably succeed such a villanous Attempt, thought the only way to shift off the Calumny, was to turn the Machination into publick ridicule, to invalidate the sincerity of those Accounts wherein the same had been represented; by insinuating, in their Papers, as well as verbal Controversies, that the Quills of Wildfire and the Inkhorn Implements, made the Plot look like the arch Contrivance of some unlucky School Boys. In answer to, which, had the Design indeed been level'd at some Botcher or Cobler, who, by reason of their sitting in open Stalls, have too often occasion to complain to their Parents and School-Masters of the provoking Pranks which Mercurial Lads are apt to play with such Fellows, the Insinuation might have pass'd well enough, and the Delign been thought a Stratagem to have frighten'd a peevish Busy-body from telling Tales for the future. But why, or how, a Cabal of School-Boys, ignorant of publick Affairs, should point out one of the greatest Ministers of State in the Kingdom, and a Person at whom the Whiggish Faction level all their Malice, is difficult to the last Degree, for a Man of Reason to conceive: Belides, there was something more in the Contrivance of the Machine, than is to be found with in the reach of such Green Capacities; and such Symptoms of Revenge through out the whole Conspiracy, as could not be generated in the Hearts of Children, or unbearded Youths, against a Man of Quality, who soars in a Station so disparatively high above the Thoughts or Resentments of such callow Striplings.

That large Inkhorns, loaded with Powder and Ball, will do the Execution of a Pocket-Pistol at a small Distance, is not to be question'd: And if the Destructron of any Person be spitefully aim'd at, tho' it be with a Popgun, that will strike a Man dead, the barbarity of the Attempt spoils the Jest of the Instrument, which, tho' it be play'd with by Boys, if it be made mischievous by Men, I think the harm that is done with it, or that is but attempted by an inveterate Hand, ought not to be turn'd into Comedy, when the evil Intent of those that use it is to act a Tragedy upon another, if by their own Care they avoid not the Misfortune. It is therefore, the Opinion of most impartial Persons, that the Whiggish Contrivers of the aforemention'd Machine, had the subtilty to make choice of the most Boyish Instruments they could pitch on for their daring Work; yet such that might answer their purpose as effectually, as those more commonly employ'd upon such desperate Occasions, that in case an Accident should obstruct the End propos'd, they might have a larger Scope, and a more plausible Pretence to turn the tragical Attempt into a Coffee-House Farce; and by ridiculing the Implements concern'd therein, perswade the World to believe there was no thing in it; or, that if there was, it was only the maggotty Contrivance of some whimsical Person, who was merrily dispos'd to give his Lordship an Amusement; and that instead of being magnify'd into a Plot, it ought rather to be laugh'd at: But this, alas, is such transparent Policy, which the Whigs have us'd so very often, since their Bear-Garden Managers were so fatally disappointed by Dr. *Sacheverel*, that they have worn it threadbare; therefore if their scribling Votaries think it a sufficient Argument of their Party's Innocence, and that because the Coverlets of their late ill Designs have been frequently us'd upon other Occasions, nothing ought to be suspected that is hid under them, in my Opinion they are but weak Advocates, for the same Cloak that hangs to Day up on an honest Man's Shoulders, may muffle up a Rogue to Morrow, and hide the Dagger-Hand-of some nefarious Ruffian, who has Murder in agitation: So that tho Puppit-shows and Bonfires heretofore have been thought necessary Artifices to inflame the People against the Pope and the Devil, yet that is no reason why an angry Faction hould challenge the Privilege of exaspe rating the Rabble against the Church and Government by the like Practises: And tho' Inkhorn-Guns are us'd by Schoolboys, to please their Childishness upon a Bonfire Day, yet it does not follow, that when the same are converted to so villanous a purpose as they were of late, that therefore the Design, because it miscarry'd, was only worthy to be made a Jest, and ought not to be look'd upon as a Whiggish Contrivance; but rather a Schoolboy's Project: For, in my Opinion, 'twas a *true-blue Protestan Gun-Powder-Treason-Plot*, as much as that which is remember'd on the Fifth of *November* was a *Popish* one. But, GOD be thank'd, both sail'd, and the Whigs have as little Success to brag of, in their late Conspiracies as the Papists had to boast of in any of their former.

A Poem Alluding to the Plots and Conspiracies of the Whiggish Faction

Inspir'd by Lucifer they cannot test
Whilst any Monarch rules the British Throne,
But think themselves much injur'd and opprest
If any Pow'r's superior to their own.
That makes em strive to low'r the Diadem,
And trample down the Church that guards the Crown;
For they'd have Kings accountable to them,
But they themselves accountable to none.
Pride is the Sire and Avarice the Dam
Of all the ill Designs they have in hand,
Wealth and Dominion are alone their Aim,
For those they sacrifice their native Land.
To that good End they did the War prolong,
And drein'd tie bleeding Nation of her Coin,
Hoping in time to be so rich and strong,
That they by force might finish their design.
To make themselves sole Masters of the whole,
The Factious Party do their Genius bend,
Cry Reformation, but attempt the Rule,
Thither do all their pious Clamours tend.
For could they into th' Church but introduce
Those Innovations at *Geneva* coin'd,
The Saints would soon, according to their use,
Their lawful Kings in Iron Fetters bind,
For that their Managers appear'd so warm
Against Sachev'rel's Doctrine at St. *Paul*'s,

In hopes, by kindling a Rebellious Storm,
They might once more prophane those sacred Walls,
But Providence inspir'd the pious Queen
With Courage to approve such Instruments
That in the nick of Danger step'd between
Their black Endeavours and their wish'd
By whom the doubtful ballance soon was turn'd,
Their hopes defeated and their Party Tools,
By all the Nation ridicul'd and scorn'd,
As ill-designing Knaves or busy Fools,
The Ropes untwisted they had long prepar'd,
To bind the Jaws and clutches of the Laws.
The Queen allarm'd to stand upon her guard,
And the Church arm'd against the Good Old-Cause.
The Party cast like fallen Angels down,
From all their boasted and mismanag'd Pow'r,
Despis'd and slighted by the angry Throne,
And shut, like Traytors, out the Presence Door.
These are the just returns of their Intrigues,
Which make the sinking Faction snarl and grin,
And aim at *Dutch* and *Hannoverian* Leagues,
To check the peaceful measures of the Queen.
These are the Scourges that perplex the Saints,
And raise their old rebellious Fury high,
Who never fail of Plots in their defence,

When other Machinations go awry.
From hence the Waxwork Puppits first arose,
The Mohocks, Bandbox, Courtships of the
But all the Schemes the Party could compose,
Were too ill manag'd to be brought about.
May all their Projets, factiously design'd,
Meet with the like Success, for if the Knaves
Should gain the point they aim at we should find
The Church worse treated than *Virginia* Slaves.

Select Observations of the Whigs Policy and Conduct in and Out of Power

To be mercenary, oppressive, and imperious in Power, they hold infallibly necessary, that thereby they may inrich themselves, impoverish their Adversaries, and awe the Prince from wresting the Authority out of their griping Hands upon any private Whispers of their Male-Administration.

To be insatiably craving of a bountiful Prince, they think their best Security, that by keeping him Poor, and making them selves Rich, they may be the better able, when he sees his Error, and has done Giving, to attempt what he refuses, by open Force and Rebellion.

To make the Right of Kings depend upon the People, is a Flattery to the Crowd, by which they have ever, till of late, united the Rabble to their Factious Party; that when they were desirous to awe the Crown into unreasonable Compliances, they might raise Tumults to alarm the Government, and fright the Ignorant with the cries of *Popery and Slavery*, whilst themselves are hatching some Fanatical Plot or other to overthrow the Constitution.

When they cry out for War it is in order to precipitate the Government into Straits, that if their Party are strong enough in the House of Commons, which't struggle to make so upon such Occasions, they may advance Grievances, and curtail the Prerogative upon every Supply, and, like greedy Usurers, make immoderate Advantage of the Crown's Necessities.

Nor will any War content 'em but with *France*, which is principally owing to the Whigs aversion to Monarchy, and their great Approbation of a Commonwealth; therefore they take a pleasure in setting Kingdoms together by the Ears, that one Crown'd-Head may be the destruction of another; whilst the *Dutch* and themselves make Advantages of the Quarrel. And when by treacherous Means they have advanc'd their Prosperity to a remarkable height, preach it up among the Ignorant as a special Mark of GOD's peculiar Favour to that Reform'd Nation, the better to perswade the common People of Britain to flight Kingly Power, and to have a greater Veneration for Dutch Government. *From which, Good Lord deliver us.*

Whenever they have a mischievous Design in agitation, which they are seldom without, to prevent Suspicion, they never fail to charge a parallel Plot upon the Church, that (Jugler-like) whilst they play their Trick they may turn the Eyes of the Multitude the wrong way. To this end they cry'd out *Popery* and the *Pretender*, when themselves were setting up Protector *John* according to Revolution-Principles; for the same reason they continue to cry, *The Pretender's coming*, when them selves are contriving to bring over some body else before their time. And, rather than lose the opportunity of Revenge, would all turn *Jacobites* in Rebellion to Her Majesty, if they could but promise themselves Success, and the Gentleman that pretends had but Faith enough to trust them.

Tho' they love Plotting as dearly as a Jilt does Intriguing, yet now they are out of Power they are very cautious how they venture their Necks to accomplish their Designs; which shews, the Riches that made them insolent in Authority, makes them Cowards now they have forfeited their Posts; for all their tottering Schemes are so faintly erected with a shaking Hand, that every breath of Government brings them to the Ground and buries the Foundations of their Plots in their own Ruins.

They are blustering Pilots in fair Weather, and care not whither they steer, if a Golden Shore be but the end of their Voyage: But when a Storm blows in their Teeth, and they have nothing on their Backs but Rocks and Shelves, tho' they fire their Guns, and make a roaring noise to signify their Distress, yet they have more Cunningthan to make the Danger greater by their Foolhardiness, now they have lost the Mob, their only Hope and Anchor. Therefore there is no Danger to be apprehended from a Whiggish Plot, so long as their Party are out of Power, and the common People their Enemies.

When they are most loud and noisy, like Town-Bullies, they are the least to be fear'd; for they always threaten with the greatest vehemence, when it is least in their Power to do Hurt; and, like the deepest Waters, carry the smoothest Countenance when they are secretly working some profound Design that has Mischief in the bottom.

When they have Power in their Hands they always seem to despise those Enemies they fear most, in hopes their contempt may make their Adversaries desperate, and provoke 'em to attempt some extravagant Enterprize that may bring them into the reach of a Whig Junco in Authority, to compleat their ruine.

Neither their Politicks nor their Natures will admit of Mercy to an Opposite, when they have Power to crush him; for, of the two, they hold it less Criminal to hang a Friend than to save an Enemy.

It is always a Rule with them, to fix odious Appellations upon whatever makes against 'em, and to improve and illustrate whatever makes for 'em with better Names than it deserves; as for Instance, a Parliamentary Dispensation of the Penal Laws they could call an Act of Toleration, be cause it much concern'd their Interest to make the best of so kind an Indulgence: But the *Utretcht* Negotiation[11] they could impudently style a Fellonious Treaty, be cause they knew that Peace would be the ruin of their Measures.

To conclude, they are too fiery to Govern, and too stubborn to Obey, and so oppressive and irregular when invested with Authority; that whenever the Churchmen have a mind to beat the Whigs out of Play, they need no other Weapons than the open Examples of that inveterate Party.

11 At the Congress of Utrecht, which opened on 29 January 1712, and led to the Peace of Utrecht, signed between 1713 and 1715 by Louis XIV of France, Philip V of Spain, Queen Anne (of Great Britain), Charles VI (Holy Roman Emperor), Frederick William I of Prussia, John V of Portugal, States General of the Dutch Republic, and Victor Amadeus II of Sardinia—the belligerents in the War of Spanish Succession. —Ed.

The CHARACTER OF A *Calves'-Head Club* Man

e is the Spawn of a Regicide, hammer'd out of a rank *Anabaptist* Hypocrite; his father was enabled to beget him by the Fat of sequestered Lands, upon a Bed stollen from an honest Cavalier. His villanous Principles he imbib'd in his Mothers Womb, nourish'd them, when Born, with her infectious Milk, and is an incorrigible Rebel by instinct of Nature, improv'd into an incarnate Devil by the early Infusions of his Nurse, which were ripen'd to Maturity by a malicious Education. He is harden'd in his Hatred to Kings and Bishops, beyond the Influence of Grace, or Check of Conscience; and thinks nothing can be a more meritorious Act, than to sacrifice either to the Fury of a mad Rabble, who, when they have but Liberty and Property in their Mouths, always let loose the Devil in their Hearts, and believe the very Name of the Protestant Religion, gives a Sanction to their Villanies. He is a Republican Monster, so full of Passion and Prejudice, that he is blind to all Truth, and deaf to all Reason; and is so cursedly obstinate in the justification of his own Errors, that it is as easy a matter for a Man to take an Elephant by the Snout, and throw him over his Back, as a Fox does a Goose, as it is to convince him of any Truth started in Opposition to his own partial Sentiments. When he talks about Religion or Government, it is generally with as much Violence as a Fish-Woman Scolds; and the Wise-Men of *Gotham* might as well have hedg'd in their *Cukkov*, as a Man confine him within the Bounds of good Manners. When he disputes his Principles, he is as hot as Pepper, as biting as Mustard, and as sour as Vinegar. He always talks as impudently of Great Men, as if they were his Fellows, and snuffs up his Nose at the Name of a King, as if the very Title itself was grown offensive to his Nostrils. He cannot speak with Respect towards any Government, but a Common-Wealth; and if you do but say one Word in behalf of the Court or its Favourites in his Company, he would, with more Patience, hear you speak twice as much in the Praise of the Devil; for it is a Maxim among such Rebels, (*viz.*) That all Kings are Tyrants, and their Favourites Betrayers of their Country. His chiefest Recreation is, to invent false Calumnies; and his greatest Industry is to spread them when he has done. His Darts are always levell'd at those worthy Persons, who are most difficult to be hit, which is one great Reason, why his Malice is so often disappointed. He commonly accuses his Enemies of his own Evils, and measures out their Corn by the deceitful Bushel that belongs to his own Party. The most daring Hypocrite of his Associates, is always cry'd up as the greatest Saint; and the most virtuous and pious Enemy to their wicked Principles, must be cry'd down as a High-flyer, a Papist, and a Traytor to his Country. He is an impatient Angler, who thinks it best fishing in troubled Waters; and hates Peace and Quietness, as much as a poor Debtor does the sight of a Bayliff, or a Country-Farmer a wet Harvest. He is so deeply affected with the Memory of his Ancestors' Villany, that he longs for nothing more, than the like Opportunity of brewing his own Hands in Royal Purple, that the Son might have the satisfaction of being full as wicked as his Father. He has more wild Notions in his Head relating to Government, than a crack-Brain'd Mathematician has concerning perpetual Motion; and has more Ambition in his Breast, than the most extravagant Tyrant in the Universe. He is very fearful of being made a Slave, but is very desirous of being a Slave-maker; for whenever he cries out for Liberty, he is endeavouring to destroy it; and never thinks himself a compleat Free-man, 'till the Nation he lives in, has no Religion to guide him, no Law to punish him, and no Prince to govern him; for his chief Aim is to pull down all, when the Madness of the Common People gives him a fair Opportunity. In all Conditions, he is as restless as a froward Infant, whilst breeding of his Teeth; will please no Government, and with no Government be pleas'd. He is as tempestuous as the Ocean, that swells into Rage with every Gale that happens, and seldom reconciles himself to a Calm, 'till, like that, he has been the Occasion of some remarkable Mischief. He is one that is very swift to Revenge, but very slow to Gratitude; and like an ill-temper'd Jade, loves to run forward when he is check'd, and to hang an Arse,when he is driven. When angry, he looks as sullen, and as gloomy as a Thunder Cloud, and, like that when it breaks, makes a wonderful deal of Noise, whenever he spits his Venom. He is never better pleased than when he has got it in his Power to oppress others, which he certainly makes use of without Mercy; yet no Body bears the flightest Sufferings with so much Envy and Impatience as himself, tho' he knows in his own Conscience he has justly deserved his Punishment. He is a harsh Man to his Inferiors, and a haughty Man to his Betters; a severe Tyrant in Authority, and a turbulent Incendiary amongst Magistrates, when he is out of it. The more his Miscarriages are conniv'd at, the more impudent he grows; and the more Mercy you shew him, the less he will shew you. He is of the Nature of a Nettle, the more gently you handle him, the more apt he is to hurt you; but if ever you

Insulting, Boundless, more than any Pope.

A *Presbyter* is be that's never known
To think on any Good besides his own;
And all his Doctrine is of Hope and Faith,
For Charity, 'tis *Popery*, he saith:
And is not only silent in good Works,
But in his Practice too, resemble *Turks.*
The Churches Ornaments, the Ring of Bells,
(Can he get Pow'r) 'tis ten to one he sells;
For his well-tuned Ears can not abide
A jangling Noise, but when his Neighbours
chide.

A *Presbyter* is be, that never prays,
But all the World must hear him what he says;
And in that Fashion too, that all may see
He is an open Modern *Pharisee.*
The Name of *Sabbath* still he keeps ('tis true)
But so he is less *Christian*, more a Jew;
Nor settled Form of Prayer his Zeal will keep,
But preacheth all his purer Flock asleep:
To study what to say, where for to doubt
Of a presumed Grace to hold him out;
And to be Learned, is too Human thought;
The Apostles all (he says) were Men untaught:
And thus be proves it for the best, to be
A simple Teacher of Divinity.
The Reverence which Ceremony brings
Into the Sacred Church, his Conscience stings,
Which is so void of Grace, and so ill bent,

That kneel he will not at the Sacrament;
But sits more like a Judge, than like a Sinner,
And takes it just as he receives his Dinner,
Thus do his Saucy Postures speak his Sin,
For as without, such is his Heart within.

A *Presbyter* is he, who doth defame
Those rev'rend Ancestors from whence he came,
And, like a graceless Child, above all other,
Denies Respect unto the Church his Mother:
His Fellow-Protestants be scorns, as Men
Not sav'd, because they are not Brethen:
And lest his Doctrine should be counted new,
He wears an ancient Beard to make it true.

A *Presbyter* is he, that thinks his Place
At every Table is to say the Grace:
When the good Man, or when his Child hath
paid,
And Thanks to God for King and Realm hath
said,
He then starts up, and thinks his self a Debtor
Till he doth cry, I pray you thank God better:
When long be prays for every living thing,
But for the Catholick Church, and for the King.

A *Presbyter* is be, would wondrous fain
Be call'd Disciple by the Holy Train;
Which to be worthy of, he'll stray and err,
Ten Miles to hear a silenc'd Minister:
He loves a Vesper Sermon, hates a Mattin,

As he detests the Fathers nam'd in *Latin*.
And as he *Friday Sunday* makes in Diet,
Because the King and Canons do deny it,
The self-same Nature makes him to repair
To Week-day Lectures, more than *Sundays*
Prayer.
And as the Man must needs in all things err,
He starves his Parson, crams his Lecturer,

A *Presbyter* is be, whose Heart is bent
To cross the Kings Designs in Parliament,
Where, whilst the place of Burgess he doth
bear,
He thinks he owes but Small Allegiance there,
But stands at distance, as some big her thing,
Like a *Licurgus*, or a kind of King,
Then, as in errant Times bold Knights were
wont
To seek out Monsters, and Adventures bunt;
So with his Wit and Valour, be doth try
How the Prerogative be may defy.
This be attempts, and first be fain would know,
If that the Sovereign Power be new, or no:
Or if it were not fitter Kings should be
Confin'd unto a limited Degree;
And, for his part, likes a Plebeian State,
Where the poor Mechanicks may still debate
All matters at their Pleasure, not confin'd.
To this or that, but as they cause do find;
When, tho' that every Voice against him go,
He'll say the Giant with his single (No.)

He in his Heart, tho' at a poor Expence,
Abhors a Gift that's call'd Benevolence;
For as bis Mind, so is his Bounty bent,
And fill unto the King Malevolent.
He is the States-man, just enough precise,
The nearest Government to scandalize;
Nor, like a Drunkard, when he doth expose
In secret underneath the silent Rose,
To use his Freedom, when the Pot might bear
The Faults which closely be committed there;
But *Shimei*-like, to all the Men he meets,
He Spews bis frantick Venom in the Streets:
And tho' be says the Spirit moves him to it,
The Devil is that Spirit made him do it.

A *Presbyter* is he (else there is none)
That thinks the King will change Religion:
His doubtful Thought, like to his Moon-blind Eyes,
Makes the Beast start at every Shape be spies;
And what his fond mistaken Fancy breed,
He doth believe as firmly as the *Creed*;
From whence he doth proclaim a Fast, to all
That be allows to be Canonical:
And then be consecrates a secret Room,
Where none but the elected Sisters come;
When being met, doth Treason boldly teach,
And will not Fast and Pray, but Fast and Preach.
Then strains a Text, whereon be may relate
The Church's Danger, Discontent of State,
And hold them there so long in Fear and Doubt,

That some do think 'tis Danger to go out,
Believing, if they hear the Ceiling crack,
The Bishops are behind them at their Back;
And so they sit bewailing one another,
Each groaning Sister bowling to her Brother.

A *Presbyter* is he, has Women's Fears,
And yet will set the whole World by the Ears;
He'll rail in publick if the King deny
To let the Quarrel of the Spaniard die;
He storms to bear in France the Wars
should cease;
And that by Treaty, there should be Peace:
For sure (saith be) the Church doth Honour
want,
When 'tis not truly called Militant;
And in plain Truth, as far as I can find,
He bears the self-same Treasonable Mind
As doth the Jesuit; for tho' they be
Tongue-Enemies, in shew their Hearts agree,
And both prosessed Foes alike, consent,
Both to betray the Anointed Innocent;
For tho' their Manners differ, yet they aim
That either may the King or Kingdom maim;
The Difference is this way understood,
One in Sedition, t'other deals in Blood.
Their Characters abridg'd, if you will have,
Each seems a Saint yet either proves a Knave.

THE

Character

OF A

Modern Whig:

OR,

The *Republican* Fashion

Modern Whig, is a new Book with an old Title, at first Sight you'll expect *Hypocrisy* to be the Contents of it, but survey it well, and you'll find it made up of Impudence. Since Masks were forbid at the *Play-House*, he has taken off his, and the Woman of the Town has this to agree with him, that as she makes Application to her Clients Bare-fac'd, so does he, only the last is more indefatigable in debauching their Souls, than the first in distempering their Bodies.

His Fore-fathers in *Forty One*, are meer Pigmies in *Sedition*, to him; their Pretence was to remove evil Counsellors from their Sovereign, but he is never at rest, 'till he gets into an Employment to capacitate him to give evil Advice to his. When the *Penal Laws and Test* were in Vogue, who so violent a Church-man as he? When Toleration came in, who so cool and estrang'd from what he before was so zealous a Professor of?

Ask him his Religion, and his Answer is, it is older than the Ten Commandments but question him about those Commandments, and he cannot make up the Number for the Soul of him, since the fifth must needs slip him, because it enjoins Obedience to his Superiors. He is not for an *Aristocracy*, because he's conscious to himself, if only the best Men were to be chosen for our Rulers, he should never have a Finger in the Pye; but a *Democracy* suits him to a Hair, because of his Mob-Principles.

Though he is not qualify'd to be one of *Oliver*'s Chaplains, because he is not Rogue enough, he may serve for one of his Water-men, for to Look one way, and Row another is their Business.

He was put into a Post, under Pretence of being a Churchman, but is taught by Experience, that the ready way to keep in it, is not to be against the *Dissenters*; for some Body has said, *They are too great a Body to be disoblig'*d, and he knows he stands upon slippery Ground, while he gives not implicit Obedience to *some Body's* Orders.

He's an *Aristotelian*, though he loves the *Mammon* of Unrighteousness too much to be a Philosopher, and his Actions are sufficient Arguments to shew, that the Corruption of one thing, is the Generation of another. He's one that has been deputed by the People to make new *Laws*, and thinks it of no Consequence what becomes of the old. He's of an Al-a-mode Cut, and the very Reason that they should be of Force with him to stand up for the Church, slackens his Resolutions to defend her. She has been a Church from the Beginning; and *King Solomon's Mistress* is too antiquated for a Courtier's Embraces.

He's a pretended Stickler for the Queen's Authority, just so long as he receives the Queen's Money; while, to shew how undeserving he is of her Royal Favours, he confederates himself for the Downfal, of the Queen's Religion. He's an *English* man, with a *Scotch* Heart, an *Irish* pair of Heels, and a *Spanish* Countenance. His Courage is in chusing the strongest Side, his Constancy in being ever subject to Variation; and his Honesty, in what you think to call it, for I know not where to find it, unless it be in his Gravity.

He's for a single Ministry, that he may play the *Tom Double* under it, and had rather the Management of Affairs should be in one, than in many; because in the Multitude of Counsellors, there would be no Safety for him, and the fewer the Superintendants, the more may be the Miscarriages of those that are subordinate to them, without being discern'd. Not that he is of this Temper for any other Account, since, notwithstanding his pretended Affection to Her Majesty and Government, he leans much more towards a *Common wealth*, than a Monarchy, and had rather the Executive Power was to be entrusted with a Committee of Safety, and he to be the *Obadiah* of the Party, than to be lodg'd where it is.

He might be a *Camelion* for his different Appearances, but he knows not how to live upon Air. He's a meer *Reptile*, that should have had the Serpent for his Father, from his soliciting other People to Sin; and Eve for his mother, by his readiness to comply with Temptations himself. He was born when the Parliament Army was in an Uproar, and had a mutinous Tongue all the last Reign, but his Eye-light took away the Use of its for he no sooner saw the Apple of Preferment, but he laid hold of it, and was silent.

He's a meer *Weather-cock*, though not a High Church-man, and always faces about, and turns his Back-side upon every Wind, but what blows from the Court. He never looks upon Her Majesty's Arms, but *Semper Eadem* gives him the Gripes, for he knows he had not been what he is had he continued what he was. He's Regis ad *Exemplum* only in his Cloaths, not his Principles, and pays a greater Deference to Her Majesty's way of Dress; than Her Worship. He's the very Reverse of one of the Members of the Rump Parliament even while he sides with them that justify their Proceedings: They set aside the House of Lords as useless he's for pulling down the Authority of the House of Commons, and making a Surrendry of their Rights in one Point, that he may be taken for a Man of peaceable Dispositions in all other. He should be an *Israelite* by his mutinous Temper, at the same time as the rest of his Actions speak him to be an *Infidel*; and the only way to trace his Original to the Fountain Head, is to search for his Fore-fathers among the Male-contents in the Wilderness, where 'tis ten to one but you find them a crying Liberty and Property for the Flesh Pots of *Egypt*.

He's neither a Prophet, nor one of the Sons of the Prophets himself, though he is pointed out by the Prophet *Esaiah*, for one of those that say, *Peace, Peace, when there is no Peace*, and has always a mouthful of *Moderation* at your Service, when his Heart is full of *Intemperance and Persecution*; and he only has a value for the *Word*, because of all others in the *English* Vocabulary, it is made Use of but once in Holy Scripture.

To conclude; He may be understood, but not thoroughly defin'd, for his ill Practices are without end, and so might his Description. Wherefore I shall take my leave of him, by saying, He's like one of our fashonable things call'd *Beaux*, that has no Brains, because they are out of Date; so has he no *Honesty*. And if my Reader is in search after one that is neither *Fish*, *Flesh*, nor good *Red Herring*, that is, neith'r *Christian*, *Jew*, *Turk*, *Infidel*, or *Heretick*, limply, but has a Relish of the Leaven of all Sects complexly; here you have him at your Service, and much good may it do you with the Bargain, for I am glad to rid my Hands of him.

The END of The History of the Calves'-Head Club.

A	The: Divell	G	Cor: Holland
B	Olever: Cromwell	H	I: Iones
C	Io: Bradshaw Pres:	I	Lisle
D	Tho: Scott	K	Say
E	Coll: Harrison	L	Hugh Petters
F	Coll: Barksted	M	I: Goodwin

A

VINDICATION

of the

Royal Martyr,

King *CHARLES* I,

wherein are laid open

The Hellish Mysteries of the Old REPUBLICAN-REBELLION.

Written in the Time of the

USURPATION

by the Celebrated Mr. *BUTLER*, Author of *Hudibras*

TO THE

READER

he Publisher of this following Discourse, has thought fit to oblige the World with a piece of Curiosity; it was Penn'd above Forty Years since by the Ingenuous and Celebrated Author of *Hudibras*. The Libel, which be answers, was the Labour of one *John Cook*, Master of *Gray's-Inn*, a great Pains-taker in the Mysteries of Rebellion. To give you the Original of it, 'twas a studied Invective against the Person of King Charles the First, before the High Court of Justice (so call'd) of infamous Memory; but upon the Non-Pleading of the Royal Martyr, 'twas afterwards Metamorphos'd into a Pamphlet, with the

Specious Title of King Charles's *Case*, or an Appeal to a to all *Rational Men concerning his Tryal.* How Rational this Appeal was, maybe easily discover'd from those Numerous Fallacies and Notorious Falshoods, which our Author has detected in him, not only as to what concerns plain Matter of fact, but also in the Pamphleteer's, pretended way of Reasoning, the false Logick, and worse Law. I shall not enter into the Merits of the Cause; for, I suppose, the more Rational part of Mankind, is abundantly satisfied in the Innocence of that great Man, as to any thing that was laid to his Charge; and upon that Account, indeed, there would have been little Occasion at this time of Day to produce so great an Advocate for his Memory, but that there is risen amongst us a new Rule of the old Republican Stamp, who have reviv'd the Quarrel, and copied out the absolute and almost forgotten Scandal of our Libeller, and made it their own. The Author of Ludlow's Letters may be reckoned among the first of these, one that always set up for a Patron of Faction, and a Promoter of the *Good-Old-Cause*; but Shew'd himself most in that famous Pear, when he was one of the Tribunes of the People. I should not have made such a Digression upon this Worthy Patriot, but that I find him to intrude amongst his Friends, Mr. *Milton* and our *Libeller*, and seems to be the very Copy of their Malice, at least, though not their Wit; and for that Reason I must confess, be seems to be the least pointed at by our Answer. I shall say no more of him at present, but pass him by with the same Contempt as the Government bas wisely done: 'Tis but unseasonable Quarrelling with a Man that is Arm'd with so much Dirt, you'll be sure of that, if you have nothing else.

I need not trouble the Reader with any Harangue upon our Author, or his Book; I suppose he is no Stranger to the Honester and more Learned part of the Kingdom; and, as for the rest, 'twas their best Secuirity they were not known by him. I shall only add, that it was Mr. *Butler*'s Design to Print the Discourse himself, bad not Death prevented him; and since it has fell into the Editor's Hand, 'tis but a piece of Justice to his Memory, to let the World make their Advantage of it.

The ROYAL MARTYR VINDICATED

Against *John Cook*, and Several others, Painstakers in the Mysteries of REBELLION

Mr. *COOK*,

aving lately seen a Book of yours, which you are pleased to call, King CHARLES *his Case, or an Appeal to all Rational Men concerning his Tryal*; I was much invited to read it, by the Ingenuity promised in your Title. For having heard you Stile yourself Solicitor General for the King's dread Sovereign, and your own Honourable Client, the People; I was much taken taken with your Impartiality, that not only exempts all Rational Men from being your Clients in

this Case, in making them, by your Appeal, your Judges: For no Man, you know, can be Judge in his own Case, but acknowledge your High Court from which you appeal to all Rational Men to consist of no such: But indeed I had not read many Lines before I found mine own Error, as well as yours, and your Proceedings nothing agreeable to the plain Dealing I expected from you; for you presently fall to insult upon the Unhappiness of your undeserved Adversary, and that with so little Moderation, as if you strove to make it a Question, whether his incomparable Patience, or your own ungoverned Passion, should be the greater Wonder of Men; preposterously concluding him Guilty, before with one Syllable you had proved him so: A strange way of doing Justice; which you endeavour to make good by a strange insolent Railing, and more insolent Proceeding to the secret Counsel of Almighty God, from whence you presume to give Sentence on him; a Boldness no less impious than unjust in you, were it true, since we can never know it to be so.

But indeed it is hard to say, whether you have shewn more Malice or Vanity in this notable Declaration of yours; for the that considers the Affectation, and Fantastique Lightness of your Language, (such as *Ireland*, a Land of Ire, Bite-Sheep, for Bishops, and other such ingenious Elegancies of quibble); must needs confess it an Oratory more becoming a Fool in a Play, or *Peters* before the Rabble, than the Patrons of his Sovereign's Sovereign;

or the Gravity of that Court, which you say right wisely, shall be admir'd at the Day of Judgement. And therefore you do ill to accuse him of reading *Johnson*'s and *Shakespear*'s Plays, which it seems you have been more in yourself to much worse purpose, else you had never hit so right upon the very Dialect of their railing Advocates, in which (believe me) you have really out-acted all that they could fancy of Passionate and Ridiculous Outrage.

For certainly, Sir, I am so charitable to believe it was your Passion that imposed upon your Understanding; else, as a Gentleman, you could have never descended to such peasantry of Language, especially against such a Person, to whom (had he never been your Prince), no Law enjoins (whatsoever his Offences were) the Punishment of Ribaldry. And for the Laws of God, they absolutely Condemn it; of which I wonder you that pretend so much to be his Counsel, should be either so ignorant or forgetful.

Calamity is the Visitation of God, and (as Preachers tell us) a Favour he does to those he loves, where ever it falls, it is the Work of his Hand, and should become our Pity not our Insolence. This the Ancient Heathen knew, who believing Thunder came from the Arm of God, reverence the very Trees it lighted on.

But your Passion hath not only misled you against Civility, and Christian Charity, but Common Sense also; else you would never have driven your Chariot of Reason (as you call it) so far out of the Road, that you forget whither you are going, and run over every thing that stands in your way; I mean, your unusual way of Argument, not only against Reason, but yourself, as you do it at the first sally; Fit of raving is over, you bestow much pains to prove it one of the Fundamentals of Law, That the King is not above the Law, but the Law above the King. And this you deraign, as you call it, so far, than at length you say, the King hathnot by Law so much Power as a Justice of Peace, to commit any Man to Prison; which you would never have done, if you had considered from whom the Justice derives his Power, or in whose Name his Warrants run; else you may as well say, a Man may give that which he hath not; or prove the Moon hath more Light than the Sun, because he cannot shine by Night as the Moon doth. But you needed not have strained so hard, for this will serve you to no purpose, but to prove that which was never denied by the King himself; for if you had not a much worse Memory than Men of your Condition should have, you could not so soon have forgotten that immediately after the reading of that Charge, the King demanded of your High Court, by what Law they could fit to judge him; (as offering to submit if they could produce any), but then Silence or Interuption were thought the best ways of confessing there was no such thing: And when he undertook to shew them both Law and Reason too, why they could not do it, the Righteous President told him plainly, he must have neither Law nor Reason, which was certainly (as you have it very finely) the most comprehensive, impartial, and glorious piece of Justice, that ever was played on the Theatre of *England*; for what could any Court do more than rather condemn it itself than injure Truth?

But you had better have left this whole Business of the Law out of your Appeal to all Rational Men, who can make no use of it, but against your self; for if the Law be above the King, much more is it above the Subject. And if it be so heinous a Crime in a King, to endeavour to set himself above Law, is it much more heinous for Subjects to set themselves above King and Law both. Thus, like right Mountebanks, you are fain to Wound and Poyson yourselves to cheat others, who cannot but wonder at the Confidence of your Imposture, that are not a sham'd to magnify the Power of the Law, while you violate it and confess you set yourselves really above the Law, to condemn the King for but intending it.

And indeed, Intentions and Designs are the most considerable part both of your Accusations and Proofs, some of which you are fain to fetch a great way off, as far as his Coronation Oath, which you next say, He, or the Archbishops, by his Order, emasculated, and left out very material, Words (which the People shall choose) which is most false; for these words were not left out, but rendred with more Sense (which the Commonalty have), and if you consider what they relate to (Customs) you will find you cannot, without open Injury, interpret (*elegerit* in the Latin Oath) *shall choose*: not *hath chosen*; for if you will have *consuetudines quas vulgas elegerit*, to mean *Customs*, which are to be not only use, which must be of ten repeated before it become a Custom, bur *choice* which necessarily preceeds *use*.

But suppose it were as you would have it, I cannot see with what reason you can presume it to be a design to subvert the Laws, since you know he had sworn to defend them before in the first Article of the Oath; from which I wonder how you can suppose that so wife a Prince (as you acknowledge him to be) could be so irrational to believe himself Absolute by this Omission. But you are not without further Contradiction yet, for if he were so perfidious a Violater of Oaths, as you would have the World believe, what reason had he to be so conscientious of taking them? Certainly he hath little cause to be nice what Oaths he takes, that hath no regard what Oath she breaks.

Nor can I possibly understand your other Construction of his refusal to take the Oath, as his Predecessors had done, which you will have a design: to refuse his assent to such good Laws rather than bad Ones, as the Parliament should tender; for besides the absurd Conceits that he must still like the bad better than the good, if you consider what you've afterwards, the charitable Sense will appear, by your own words, to be truest; for you confess he gave his assent to any bad one else you had not been fain, for want of such, to accuse him of a few good ones, as you do there, which of these is most probable, let every rational Christian judge.

Your next Argument, to prove the King's design to destroy the Law, is thus ordered. Those Knights that were by an old Statute to attend at the Kings Coronation, being promised by his Proclamation (in regard of the Infection then spread through the Kingdom) a Dispensation for their Absence, were after fined at the Council Table; no doubt by the Procurement of some of your own Tribe, where they pleading the Proclamation for their Indemnity were answered, That the Law of the Land was above any Proclamation: Your Conclusion is therefore, The King had a Design to subvert the Laws: Sure there is no Man in his Wits, but would conclude the contrary; such Arguments as these are much like the Ropes that *Oænus* twisted only for Asses to devour.

But if this should fail, you know you were provided with another not less substantial, and that is, his Alteration of the Judges Commissions, who heretofore had their Places granted to them during their Good Behaviour, but he made them but during Pleasure; of this you make a sad Business of a very imaginary evil Consequence; but if you had considered before what you say presently after, That the King, and not the Judges, is to be accountable for the Injustice and Oppression of the Government, &c. you would have found it very just, that he should use his Pleasure in their Dismission as well as Choice; for Men of your Profession, that have lived long enough to be Judges, are not such Punies in cunning, to play their Feats of Iniquity above-board: and if they may sit still, they can be-proved to have misbehaved themselves; the Prince that is to give account for all, may sooner know he is abused, than know how to help himself.

All the Inconveniency which you can fancy possible to ensue it, is only to such bad Judges as buy their Places; of whose Condition and loss you are very sensible, as if they had too hard a Bargain of Injustice, believe they may have Reason enough to give unjust Judgment, rather than lose their Places and their Money too, if they shall receive such Intimation from the King. But you forget yourself, when you put this in your Appeal to all Rational Men; for they will tell you, this was a bold Affront done to your High Court of Justice: For if it were potential Tyranny (as you will have, it) in the King to have but a Design to endure the Judges to give Sentence against the Law, which you say brings the People the very next Step to Slavery; What is it in those who presume to give Sentence them selves, not only contrary to Law, but the declared Opinion of all the Judges and those of their choosing too? And (I beseech you) whither, by your own Doctrine, does this bring the People that submit to it? Certainly, if you that can accuse the King of this had been a Jew heretofore, you would not only have stoned your Fellows, but your Saviour too .

But if all your Arguments should miscarry, you have a Reserve left, that does (as you say) irrefragably prove the Design; what's that? He is restless to destroy Parliaments, or make them useless. Believe me, this is right *Ignotum perignotius*, excellent Consequence to prove his Design by his De sires; you should have proved his Desires first, (if you would prove his Thoughts by his Thoughts) for certainly if ever he designed it, he desired it first. You had better have concluded plainly, he did it because he designed it, for that is all one in Sense: But if I might be but half so bold with your Designs, I should with more Reason guess you have one, to make us believe your familiar Acquaintance with the secret Counsels of God, (which you so often pretended to) else certainly he has given the Desires of Men so private a Lodging, that without his own Discovery, (which you can give us no Account of you have no other way to know them. You do well, and if I may advise you, you shall give over this unlucky thing called Reason, and betake yourself wholly to Revelations.

How these Arguments might prevail with your High Court of Justice, I can not tell; but, in my Opinion, they had little Reason to thank you for this last, for while you make the King a Traytor, and prove his meer Desire to destroy the Parliament, or make it useless, a Purpose to subvert the Laws, you do but tell them what they are that have already done it, and the People what a deal of Law they are to expect hereafter. All you can justly, in your own Sense, accuse the King of, is but Discontinuance, or untimely Dissolution of Parliaments, which I wonder with what Sense you can interpret a Design to destroy the Parliaments, since all the World knows when he parted with his Power to dissolve the Parliament too. But see how doubly unjust you are; you accuse him for not calling Parliaments so often as he was bound to do by the Law, once a Year, (as you say) or oftner; but never consider how that is impossible to be done, without dissolving them as often; for doing which, notwithstanding, with so much Clamor, you condemn him. Thus you charge him with Inconsistencies, and may, with much more reason, accuse him for calling Parliaments, because if he had not call'd them, he could never have dissolved them; which is very like your way of Argument.

But much better than you commonly use for your next, (to remove an Objection out of your way) is thus mannaged: The King, and not the Judges and evil Counsellers, ought to be accountable for the Male-Administrations, Injustices, and Oppressions of the Parliament, your Reasons he made such wicked and corrupt Judges: Were they not his own Creatures? and ought not every Man to be accountable for the Work of his own Hands? Believe me, this were something, if you could prove he made them wicked, as well as Judges. But if this Plea hold, you have argued well for your honourable Clients, the People; for if they made the King, as you say they did, you have cleared him of all such horrid Crimes, Murders, and Massacres, which you take so much Pains, to no purpose, to accuse him of; and like a right Man of Law, have undone your Clients, upon whole Score you set them; Your next Business will be to prove God guilty of the Sins of wicked Men, for they are his Creatures, and the Work of his Hands, I take it. But this is your perpetual Method of doing him right, to make him sole Author and Owner of all his ill-ordered or unhappy Actions, and not allow him a share in any good Deed or Act of Grace.

And these are the Fundamentals of the Charge, only Suppositions of Intentions and Designs, which how far you have proved just or profitable, let any Man but yourself judge: The Course you take afterwards, is much worse in my opinion, for you make your own Grounds, and either not prove them at all, (which is worse) prove them upon their own bottom, as when you take upon you to state the Ground of your Wars, and prove the King to be the Cause of it, you do it thus:

The King (you say) set up his Standard of War for the Advancement and Upholding of his Personal Interest, Power, and pretended Prerogative, against the Publick Interest of common Right, Peace, and Safety. How do you prove this? Because he fought for the Militia, for a Power to call and dissolve Parliaments, a negative Voice, to make Judges, confer Honours, grant Pardons, make Corporations, inhance or debase Money, and avoid his own Grants. These you call his Personal Interest, Power, and Prerogative, which you say he fought for. Now put the Position and Proof together, and see what Sense it will make, truly none but this, That he made War for his Prerogative, because he fought for his Prerogative. Is not this fine Logick! but suppose it were Sense, how do you prove he fought for his Prerogative? To this you have not one Word to say; and why then should we rather take your Word than the King's, who pro tested he took Arms in Defence of the Protestant Religion, the Liberty of the Subject, Privileges of Parliament, and the Laws of *England*? Certainly there is no Man in his Wits, but would rather believe his Words than your Arguments, if he does but consider, that the most improbable part of all, (he protested to fight for the Defence of the Privileges of Parliament) is found by Experience to be no Parradox. How true the rest is, Time will instruct you. But yet I cannot see why we should not rather believe them, than the Pretences of the Parliament, which were more to fight in Defence of his Person, and their own Privileges; which how they have perform'd yourself can tell: But all this while you mistake your own Question, which was not the Right of the Cause, but the Cause, or (as you have it) the Occasion of the War; and if you had a Purpose to know that, Actions had been the only Guide of your Inquiry; for Intentions and Words are uncertain, and if they make no Assaults in private Quarrels, I know not why they should in publick; and therefore, since we can never agree about the Truth of more remote Causes, 'tis most just for us to place the Cause of the War where we find the first Breach of the Peace. Now, that the King was cleared of this, all indifferent Men, who had the Unhappiness to be acquainted with the Method of their own undoing, can very well testify. And if the Parliament should deny it, their own Votes would contradict them, as well as their Actions; for when they first raised Horse and Arms, they pretended to do so, because it appear'd the King, seduc'd by wicked Counsel, intended to make War against the Parliament; whereby they confess he had not then done it, and they had so little Ground to make it appear he ever would, that they were fain to usurp the Right of his Cause to justify their own; and, they say, took Arms for the Defence of the King, which, if we grant, it must follow, they first made War against him; for no Body else ever did, against whom they could possibly defend him; nor did their Actions, in offering the first Violence, less declare who began the War, when having an Army ready to invade him, before he set up his Standard, they both follow'd and set upon him, as they did at *Edge-Hill.* Go as far as you can, you will still find the *Scots* (whose Quarrel the Parliament took up at the second hand, as well as they followed their Examples) were the first Beginners of all.

This being granted, how the King could afterwards do less than he did, I cannot understand: *First,* he was bound by the Law of Nature (which you say is Legislative, and hath a suspensive Power over all Human Laws) to defend himself. *Secondly,* By his Coronarion-Oath, which he took to keep the

Peace. And how could he do that, but by his raising Power to suppress those who had already broken it? *Thirdly*, By the Laws of the Land, which, you say, trusted him with the Power of the Sword: And how could he preserve that Trust, if he had sate still, and suffer'd others not only to take it from him, but to use it against him.

But it is most probable that he never to let them be before-hand with him, in seizing upon his Castles, Magazines, and Ships; for which there can be no Reason imagin'd, but that he was to give them any Occasion (in securing them) to suspect he did but intend a War. And by all this I doubt not but it appears plain enough to all Rational Men, that he was loath, so far from being the Cause of the War, that he rather fell into it by avoiding it; and that he avoided it so long, 'till he was fain to take Arms at so great a Disadvantage, as he had almost as good have sate still and suffered. And in this you have used the King with the same Justice the Christians receiv'd from *Nero*, who having set *Rome* on fire himself, a Sacrifice to his own wicked Genius, laid the Odium of it on the Christians, and put them to Death for it.

But this Way you found too fair and open for your Purpose, and therefore declin'd it, for having prov'd his Intentions by his Desires, and his Actions by his Intentions, you attempt a more preposterous way yet, to prove both; by what might have been his Intentions: And to this purpose, you have the Confidence (in spight of Sense) to make Contingencies the final Cause of Things; and impolitick Accidental, possible Inconveniences (which all the Wit of Man can never avoid) the intended Reasons of State. As when you will have the King fight for the Militia, only to command the Purse of the People; for a Power to make Judges, only to wrest the Laws; to grant Pardons, that Publick-spirited Men, as you call them, may be made away, and the Murderers Pardon'd, &c. All which being Creatures of your own Fancy and Malice, (and no part of his Quarrel) you are so far from proving he fought for that; when you have I train'd your Ability, all you can say is but this, in your own Sense, That he fought for a Power to do that, which he never would do when it was in his Power: But if you take this Liberty, I cannot but think how you would bestir yourself, if you could ' but get your GOD, as you have done your King, before such an impartial High Court of Justice as this! how would you charge him with his Misgovernment in Nature, for which, by the very same Logick, you may prove He made us all Slaves, in causing the Weaker to hold his Life at the pleasure of the Stronger; that He set up a Sun to dazle our Eyes, that we might not see; and to kindle Fevers in our Veins, made Fire to burn us, Water to drown us, and Air to poison us, and then demand Justice against him; all which you may easily do, now you have the trick on't, for the very same Reason will serve again, and with much more Probability; for 'tis easier to prove, that Men have been burnt, and drowned, and died of the Plague, than to make it appear the King ever used your finer Device to remove Publick-spirited Men; or can you, without extreme Injustice, suppose he ever would? For 'tis so much as very well known, he highly favour'd and advanc'd his greatest Opposers, (for such you mean, I know) whom he found Owners of any eminent Desert, as he did the Earl of *Strafford*, and the Attorney-General *Noy*, (and for other honest Men, as you will have them) whom Frenzy or Sedition set against him, by your own Confession; he did not suffer those black Stars (very strange ones) to slit their Noses, and crop their Ears.

But now I think of these honest publick spirited Men, certainly some of them have not so good an Opinion of the Honesty of your publick Proceedings, but they would willingly venture not only their Ears again, (if they had them) but their Heads too, in Defiance of your most comprehensive piece of Justice, whose Cause, while you take upon you to plead against their Consent, as you have done your honourable Clients the People; you deserve in reason to be thrown over the Bar by your own Party; for you but confess your own Injustice, while you acknowledge the publick Honesty of those that oppose it.

How solid or pertinent those Arguments of yours have have been been, let any Man that is sober, judge: But you are resolved, right or wrong, they shall pass, to let us know how easily he that has the Unhappiness to be judged by his Enemies, is found guilty of any thing they please to lay to his Charge; and therefore satisfied with your own Evidence, you proceed to Sentence and Condemn the King with much Frailty, by the fundamental Laws of this Kingdom, by the general Law of all Nations, and the unanimous Consent of all rational Men in the World, for imploying the Power of the Sword to the Destruction of the People, with which they entrusted him for their own Protection. How you got the Consent of Rational Men to this sentence, I can not imagine; for 'tis most certain, (by your own Confession) that he never imployed the Sword, but against those who first fought to deprive him of it, and, by that very As, declared they did not trust him, and consequently absolved him both from the Obligation that he had to protect them, and the Possibility too: For no Man can defend another longer than he defends himself; so that if you will have your Sentence to be just, you must confess it to be Non sense for you must not only prove, that those who fought against him were the People that trusted him; not those who fought for him, but the lesser, or less considerable part of the People, the People as you have Confidence to call your honourable Clients, being not the twentieth part of the very Rabble; which if you can do, you are much wiser than *Solomon*. For it is easier to divide a Child into two parts, make one of those two parts a whole Child; and if you have the trick on't, you shall be next allow'd to prove, That take four out of six, there remains six: Nor is there more Justice or Reason in the Sentence, than in the

Course you take to uphold it; for while you deny the old Maxim of Law, *That the King can do no Wrong*, you maintain a new one much worse, *That be may Suffer any*; and having limited his Power to act only according to Law, expose him to suffer, not only without, but against Law. Truly it is hard Measure, but rather than fail of your purpose, you will make as bold with Scriptures as you have done with Reason, if it stand in your way; as you do when you interpret that place of the Apostles, *Where no Law is, there is no Transgression*, to mean, where there is neither Law of God, nor Nature, nor positive Law: I wonder where that is; certainly, you had better undertake to find out a Plantation for *Archimedes* his Engines to move the Earth, than but fancy where that can be, which you must do before you can make this Scripture to be understood to your purpose; and I cannot but smile to think, how hard a Talk that will be for such a strong Fancy as yours, that cannot conceive what yourself affirm; for when you deny it possible to suppose two supreme Powers in one Nation, you forget that you had acknowledged much more before for you confess the King to be supreme, when you say very elegantly, he made Head against the Parliament, who acknowledged him to be the Head thereof; and yet you say the Parliament is the Supreme Authority of the Nation. Thus you affirm that really to be, which you think is impossible to imagine.

But such lucky Contradictions of yourself, as well as Sense, are as familiar with you as Railing;

for besides the many before mentioned, and your common Incongruities of Speech is as far from Construction as the Purpose; there are others, which for your Encouragement ought not to be omitted; and when you would prove the King the most abominable Tyrant that ever People suffer'd under, yet you say he was beloved of some, and feared abroad: His Judges you compared to the Saints sitting in Judgment at the last Day, and yet by your own Doctrine, they are more like Bears and Wolves, in sitting by a Commission of Force; their High Court is a Royal Palace of the Principles of Freedom; and yet, till the People voluntarily submit to a Government (which they never did to the Authority of that) they were but Slaves. The Parliament, you say, petition'd the King as good Subjects; and yet immediately after you make them his Lords, and himself Servant; so they give him the Honour of his own Royal Assent, and yet they often petition'd him for it. His Tryal you call most Impartial, and yet cannot deny all his Judges to be Parties, and his profest Enemies. But you hit pretty right when you say he caused more Protestant Blood to be shed than ever was spilt, either by *Rome*, Heathen, or Antichristian; for grant that partly to be true, and confess as much Protestant Blood as ever was spilt by the Heathen *Romans*, unless they could kill Protestants Eight-hundred Years before there were any in the World, which eloquent piece of Nonsense we must impute to your Ignorance in Chronology, or Confusion of Notion, which you please. Nor are those Riddles of Contradiction only in your Words, but in the whole Course of your Proceedings, for you never do the King any Right, but where you do him the greatest Wrong; and are there only rational, where you are most inhumane, as in your additional Accusations since his Death; for there you undertake to prove something, and give your Reasons, (such as they are) to make it appear, which were fair Play, if you do not take an Advantage too unreasonable, to argue with the Dead. But your other Impeachments consist only of Generals, prove nothing, or Intentions, which can never be proved, or your own forc'd Constructions of Actions, or what might have been Actions, but never were; all which you only aggravate with Impertinency and foul Language, but never undertake to prove; and if we should grant all you would say, and suppose you said it in Sense or Order, it would serve you to no purpose, unless you have by Proof or Argument applied it to him, which you never went about to do.

But if this were the worst, you might be born with, as a thing more becoming the Contempt, than the Anger of Men; but who can preserve any Patience, that does but think upon that Prodigy of your Injustice, as well as Inhumanity, to accuse the King after his Death, of what you were asham'd to charge him with when alive? For what you say concerning the Death of King James, you will become the Scorn of your own Party, for they never used it farther than they found it of Advantage to some Design they had in hand; as when they would move the King to grant their Propositions, they made it serve for an Argument to him, *If he would Sign, be should be fill their Gracious King*; if not, *He killed his Father*: But when they found he would not be convinced of such Logick, they laid it utterly aside; for, without doubt, they had not lost an Advantage so useful as they might have made it in the Charge, had they not known it would have cost them more Impudence to maintain, than they should need to use in proceeding without it; but let us consider your Student's Might, with which you first say you are satisfied, and yet after have it as a Riddle. First, he was observ'd to hate the Duke, but instantly, upon the Death of King *James*, took him into his special Grace and Favour, of which you conceive this Art must be the Cause. Believe me, your Conjecture is contrary to all Experience, and the common Manner of Princes, who use to love the Treason, but hate the Traytor; and if he had been so politick a Tyrant as you would describe him, he would never believe his Life safe, nor his Kingdom his own, while any Man lived, (much less his Enemy, whom such a King would never trust) of whose Gift and Secresy he held them both; nor is it likely that he who would not spare the Life of his Father to gain a Kingdom, should spare the Life of his Enemy to secure it. As for his Dissolving the Parliament, I believe not only all Wise Men, but all that ever heard of this, will acquit him; whether he did it to avoid the Duke's Impeachment you cannot prove, but if you could, you must consider, that in such Cases, Princes may as well protect their Favourites from Injury as Justice, since no Innocence can serve them, if they lie as open to the Question, as they do to the Envy of Men.

But for the better Satisfaction of those you appeal to, I shall add this; It is most certain that this Humour of Innovation began to stir in the first Parliament of this King, and grew to an Itch in the Commons for the Alteration of Government; to which end, they first resolved to pull down the chief Instrument thereof, the Duke of *Buckingham*: But having then no *Scotch* Army, nor Act of Continuance to assure their Sitting, all the Wit of Malice could never invent more politick Course than to Impeach him, and to put this Article (true or false) into his Charge; for thus they were not only sure of the Affections of the People, who, out of the common Fate of Favourites, generally hated the Duke, and are always pleased with the Ruin of their Superiors, but secured from the King's Interposition, whom they believed, by this means, bound up from protecting the Duke, (though he knew his Innocency) left the Envy and Fancy of al should fall upon himself; but the King, who understood their Meaning, and knew this was but in order to their further Attempts, (which always begin with such Sacrifices) suddenly dissolved the Parliament, and by his Wisdom and Policy, kept that Calamity sixteen Years after from the People, which the very same Courses and Fate of these unhappy Times have since brought upon them. But you have taken more Pains to prove him Guilty since his Death, of the Rebellion in *Ireland*, altho' with as little Reason or Ingenuity, only you deal fairly in the Beginning, and tell us what Judgment and Caution we are to expect from you, when you say, as a Ground for all your Proofs, *If you meet a Man running down Stairs, with a bloody Sword in bis Hand, and find a Man stabbed in the Chamber, though you did not see this Man run into the Body by that Man which you met; yet if you were of the Jury, you durst not but find him guilty of the Murther*. I hope not, before you know whether the Man killed were sent by the King to fetch the Man you met, for then you may say it must be in his own Defence: Truly you are a subtil Enquirer, but let us hear some of the clear Proofs; first, he durst never deny it absolutely; besides the less to imagine, that he who had Wickedness enough to commit so horrid an Act, should have the innocent Modesty not to deny it, when he durst not own it. He sent Thanks to *Muskerry* and *Plunket* by *Ormond*, which you are confident his Height of Spirit would never have done, if he had not been as guilty as themselves; and may not *Ormond*, that carried the Thanks, be, by the same Reason, as well proved guilty as the King? What's next, If he had not been guilty, he would have made a thousand Declarations, and have sent to all Princes in the World for Assistance against such Hell hounds and Blood-hounds, &c. That was impossible to be done without fending to the Pope, and then you would have proved it clear indeed. But the Copy of his Commission to the *Irish* Rebels, is in the Hands of the Parliament. 'Tis most certain, they never believed it themselves, else it had not been omitted in the Charge. But now for an Argument to the purpose; after the *Irish* were proclaimed Traytors and Rebels by the King, their General Council made an Oath to bear true and faithful Allegiance to King *Charles*, and by all means to maintain his Royal Prerogative against the Puritans in the Parliament of *England*, which they would never have done, unless he had commanded or consented to the Rebellion: But observe then what will follow; after the two Houses at Westminster were proclaimed Rebels and Traytors by the King, they made a solemn Covenant to defend his Royal Person, Rights and Dignities, against all Opposers whatsoever; and therefore by the same Reason he did command or consent to the War raised by the Parliament raised against himself. But did they not say they had his Commission, and call themselves the King and Queen's Armies? But then, you forgot who they were that said so, Hell hounds, and Blood-hounds, Fiends and Fire-brands, and bloody Devils, not to be named without Fire and Brimstone; do you think such are not to be believed, (especially when they speak for their own Advantage) rather than the People of God, the faithful of the Land at *Westminster*, who likewise, when they raised Forces, said, they did it for the King and Parliament? Can any Man in his Wits deny but the King is to be believed before either of these? And yet you cannot be perswaded, but his Offer to go in Person to suppress the Rebellion, was a Design to return at the Head of 20 or 30000 Rebels to have destroyed this Nation; that's very strange! but first, how shall we believe what you fay before, (to shew your Breeding?) Never was Bear so unwillingly brought to the Stake, as he to declare against the Rebels, if he offered to adventure his Person to suppress them: When you made this agree in Sense, let us know how you can suppose the same Person, the wisest King in Christendom, and yet so foolish to study his own Destruction; for who could suffer so much in the Ruin of this Nation as himself? For his hindering the Earl of *Leicester*'s going into *Ireland*,[1] he had much more Reason to do so, than the Parliament had to hinder him, and therefore you may as well conclude guilty, as him, of the Rebellion.

That he sold or exchang'd for Arms and Ammunition the Cloath and Provisions sent by the Parliament to the Protestants in *Ireland*, you must either accuse the Parliament, which seiz'd upon his Arms first, and used them against him, or prove them above the Law of Nature, (which I believe you had rather do) that commands every Man to defend himself. But the Rebels in *Ireland* gave Letters of Mart[2] for taking the Parliament's Ships, but freed

1 The Earl of Leicester was named Lord Lieutenant of Ireland on 14 June 1641. —Ed.

2 An authority formerly issued to private adventurers in time of war empowering them to seize the ships and goods of enemy

the King's as their very good Friends. I see you are not such a Wizard at Designs as you pretend to be; for if this be the deepest Reach of *Rome*, when *Hannibal* invaded *Italy*, and burnt all the Country of the *Roman* Dictator, you would have spared no longer to have proved him Confederate with the Enemy. But I fear I may seem as vain as yourself in repeating your Impertinencies. There is one Argment that would have serv'd instead of all to convince you of Wickedness and Folly in this Business, and that . is the Silence of the Charge, which, by your own Rule, ought to betaken (*pro confesso*) there was never any such thing.

I will not trouble my self nor any Body with your *French* Legend, as being too in considerable to deserve any serious Notice, built only upon Relations and Hear-says, and proved with your own Conjectures, which, how far we are to credit from a Man of so much Byass and Mistakes, any of those you appeal to, shall determine, to whom I shall say but this, that you do but acknowledge the Injustice of the Sentence, while you strove to make it good with such Additions; for if you had not believed it very bad, you would never have taken so much Pains to mend it: And I hope your High Court will punish you for it, whose Reputation your officious Indiscretion hath much impaired to no purpose: For tho'we should grant all your Additions to be true, as you would have it, it does not at all justify the King's Death, since he did not Die in Relation

---

subjects. —Ed.

to any thing there objected; and all you can possibly aim at by this pitiful Argument, is but to prove him guilty, because he was punished; for you can never prove him punished, because he was guilty.

For your Epilogue, I have so much Charity to believe it, being of a different Thread of Language, none of your own; but either penn'd for you by your Musty *Peters*,[3] or else you writ Short-hand very well to copy after the Speech of his Tongue. How ever you came by it, sure I am it could come from no Body else; and having said so, I hope I shall need to say no more; for I shall be loath to commit the Sin of repeating any of it: But since 'tis but a Frippery of common places of Pulpit-Railing, ill put together, that pretend only to Passion, I am content you should use them yourself, and be allowed to say any thing with as little regard, as if you wore your Priviledge: Yet left you should grow so conceited as to believe yourself, I will take *Solomon*'s Advice, and answer you not in your own way of Railing or Falshood, but in doing some Right to Truth, and the Memory of the Dead, which you have equally injured.

3 Hugh Peters (1598 - 1660), a preacher who supported Parliament against the King, was known for his flamboyant preaching style, which he put in service to the Puritans. —Ed.

Index

M

N

O

P

Q

R

S